Just Mission

Just Mission

Barbara and Tom Butler

MOWBRAY

Mowbray
A Cassell imprint
Villiers House, 41/47 Strand, London WC2N 5JE
378 Park Avenue South, New York, NY 10016–8810

First published 1993

British Library Cataloguing-in-Publication Data
A catalogue record for this book is available from the British Library.

Library of Congress Cataloging-in-Publication Data
Available from the Library of Congress.

ISBN 0–264–67278–X

The 'Thoughts for the Day' were originally broadcast on *Today* on BBC Radio 4.

Typeset by Colset Private Limited, Singapore
Printed and bound in Great Britain by
Biddles Ltd, Guildford and King's Lynn

Contents

Foreword

Lambeth Palace
London SE1 7JU

I commend this book most warmly, and for three good reasons.

First, it is immensely readable. Too many books about mission and evangelism are, frankly, dull. *Just Mission* sparkles with human interest and communicates directly with the reader. As you read it, you feel you are in an interesting conversation with the two authors already.

Secondly, it expands the horizon of the reader, drawing upon a wealth of experience which the Butlers have acquired in the fields of education and ministry, both in this country and elsewhere. In particular it often captures the teeming vitality of Africa, including church life in Africa, from which in this country we have so much to learn.

Thirdly, it is deliberately and effectively geared to the local church group. Almost any page of it could form the basis for a stimulating and creative discussion leading to new insights and practical action. Specific suggestions for such action are laid out at the end of each section. I welcome this heartily, for I believe that in most cases it is the local group of committed Christians which is the most effective unit for Christian mission.

I hope it will be widely used, not only as a Lent course, but generally amongst groups of Christian people in the coming years.

✠ George Cantuar:

To our children, Anna and Nicholas

Introduction

We are excited by the Church's calling to pursue the mission of God in God's world through the grace and goodness of Jesus Christ. We are frustrated that this mission is often seen in narrow and dogmatic ways. We believe that mission is history-long, worldwide, and involves every aspect of life.

Throughout our married life we have both been privileged in having the opportunity of serving the Church, but our callings have not been identical. Barbara's background has been in education and she has taught in secondary schools and colleges in both Africa and England. For the last eight years she has been the executive secretary of Christians Aware, which is ecumenical and international. Her experience has therefore been in global and local development education, mostly involving local church people in Britain and overseas. Her work has been project- and issue-orientated within the context of a Christian movement which aims to look out from itself.

Tom's experience has become increasingly involved with the institutional Anglican Church. After serving twelve years as a university chaplain in Africa and England, he has been archdeacon and bishop for the past twelve years. He has therefore a detailed knowledge of the Church's mission at parish and diocesan levels, and because he chaired the follow-up to *Faith in the City* he has a particular knowledge of urban mission. He is now Bishop of Leicester and is appreciating the opportunity to work in rural as well as urban areas. In this book we have tried to bring these various experiences together. We have found it convenient to write as 'we', although it will be obvious that we have not both shared all the experiences of which we write.

Our main aim in writing is to encourage Christians to explore and participate more fully in the Church's mission in the way which is most fruitful for them and for those they work with. We have divided the book into four main sections: 'Just Presence', 'Just Action', 'Just Witness', and 'Just Spirituality'. This order was a natural one for us personally to follow, moving from being in a place, to joining in practical action and prophecy, and to witnessing to our faith. 'Just Spirituality' is undergirding everything. If we were to draw a diagram of the sections of the book it would be circular, or of several interlocking circles, and with every aspect of mission leading to every other aspect. *Just Mission* has many aspects and many ingredients; all are necessary, all enhance all the others and all are exciting and challenging.

We have included a list of resources at the end of each section which we hope will be useful, especially for those who use the book in a study group. We have also sprinkled the book with Tom's 'Thoughts for the Day' from the *Today* programme on BBC Radio 4. These should be regarded as word-pictures or illustrations rather than an integral part of the text.

We have enjoyed writing this book and we offer it as a contribution towards the world-wide mission of the Church, which we share with our sisters and brothers all over the world.

Barbara and Tom Butler
Leicester 1992

Section One

Just Presence

Jesus had a mission—and the first thing he had to do to carry out his mission was to be here—he had to be in the world before he could change the world—he was born at a particular time in a particular place, and from living this particular life he changed lives at all times, everywhere. Likewise, before we can engage in mission of any sort we must 'be there'. The fact that Jesus shared the ordinary life of ordinary people meant that he could communicate with them mind to mind, soul to soul. Because he knew human life from the inside he had the right to speak about a renewed way of life, touched by the wonder of heaven. Any authority which Jesus of Nazareth might have had, then, did not come from any position—unlike the Sadducees he held no official position in church or state; unlike the Pharisees his authority did not come from a tradition of learning. His authority came from 'being there', being with people and being with God, sharing the life of the people in the villages and towns of Galilee, and then in his God-centred, this-worldly way, speaking naturally and power-fully about what that world might look like when renewed by God and for God. Jesus did not come with any plan or social blueprint for transforming society. He mixed with people naturally and socially, in their homes and in the countryside, listening to them and then sharing with them, opening their eyes to the God who was in them and in their world, and opening their eyes to their own special gifts and possibilities which only they could act upon. He challenged people to live from day to day, being fulfilled in their lives, and work without striving to control the future, rejoicing in whatever God had given. He opened people's eyes to the fact that God was with them in grace and judgement and, with that perspective, the world had new horizons. Our horizons are no less new, frightening, wonder-filled and challenging, and we sometimes forget that we are seeing them in ways never before available to humankind.

Soon after our marriage we went to live in Zambia in central Africa. We lived in a house on the edge of the new university campus, which was itself built on the edge of the city of Lusaka. From our veranda we could see the vastness of the African bush before us, whilst down the road we could see in one direction the fires of a traditional African village and in another the concrete towers of a modern university. We felt small, vulnerable strangers in a vast ancient and new world. One evening we were watching television when the first pictures of the earth taken from the moon were shown and, like the rest of humanity, we saw our world in a totally different way. We saw the earth as a tiny and coloured ball of light and life, floating in dark space.

That picture is now well known, but at the time it was awe-inspiring, and for us, viewing it from our situation, even more so. The African night was still in front of our eyes beyond the television screen, so what was the correct view of the earth? Was it the tiny speck of life we could see on our TV screens, a pin prick in the vastness of dark space? Or was it the enormous spread which we could see before us, with the noises of the African night? And within that African night, was the centre of gravity of life still in places like the traditional village or was it shifting to such places as the gleaming Western-style university?

All those pictures of the earth are true of course. The earth is both a tiny ball of life floating in space, and a vast collection of different places, species, cultures, and conditions. To be a human being on earth at the end of the twentieth century means to be open to all of them. Our world is like a kaleidoscope of different colours and features. As we shake the world, or the world shakes us, it arranges itself in ever different patterns. And one way or the other, shake we must.

Seeing with new eyes

'We don't inherit the world from our parents, it is on loan to us from our children.' That fact has always been true throughout human history, but we are the first generation to have the opportunity of seeing the extent and vulnerability of the world which we borrow.

Modern communications force us to be our sister's neighbour. There is no way that we can be ignorant of her, whether she lives down the road or in Calcutta. Even if we never leave our living room, the world comes to us on our TV screens, but sadly we cannot assume that this will automatically lead to international understanding, respect and co-operation. A little girl who received a book on penguins from her grandmother wrote a thank-you letter back: 'Thank you for sending me the book on penguins. I now know more about penguins than I wish to know.'

It is easy to have the same feeling about our world and our neighbours in it. It is easy for us in the West to feel like observers or victims, shaken and shrinking from contrasting cultures and faiths, from alien ways of life, from endless struggles and wars, from unimaginable poverty and from countless indescribable sufferings. One of the problems is that we all tend to see the world from inside our own places and cultures, so that when we look out it is into a mist of indiscernable and totally unappreciated shapes. We may even look in the wrong directions altogether so that the view is unnecessarily gloomy. The Gospel challenge to be a good neighbour in today's world is a challenge to learn to look through new eyes, the eyes of our neighbour, and to look in new directions towards new ways and wisdoms, new designs and understandings. The struggling, suffering world on our TV screens is our own world, and if we learn to inhabit it, to learn from it and to share with it we may discern its shape, beauty, life and hope for a future which is our own.

Modern communications not only bring the other side of the world into our living rooms. They show us the world down the road in a new way. The break up of the Soviet Union would have been unthinkable even a couple of decades ago, because then one of the levers of power was the control of information. It is far more difficult to control information today, because even the poorest families can tune in to stations on their transistor radios, and not always to 'approved' channels. People may know, therefore, what is going on in their own city or others, almost as soon as it happens. Within hours or even minutes they can be out on the streets—and in a confrontation with people who themselves are listening to the same news reports. The people of Moscow, when Russia teetered on the edge of a military coup, heard on their radios and saw on their TV screens the populist leader Boris Yeltsin standing in defiance before the tanks in front of the Parliament building, and they came out in their thousands to support him. With modern communications it is difficult for any regime in the world totally to control the flow of news to its citizens, and because of this a major weapon of totalitarian government has collapsed.

It is not only that modern communications have shrunk our world. Ease of transport now means that it is a real option for us to visit or even live and work in other parts of the world and, conversely, people originating from all parts of the world are our next-door neighbours in multi-cultural Britain. This has had enormous consequences for everyone. The global movement of people began before there was any kind of understanding of what it might mean. In the decades after the end of the Second World War British governments of all political colours responded to the fast approaching collapse of the British Empire and labour shortages by encouraging people from the new Commonwealth to come to work in Britain. And so they came in the 1950s and 1960s in considerable numbers.

Amongst them came black Christians from the Caribbean, bringing warmth and vitality to what they anticipated would be a welcoming Christian country. They were to have a shock. Colin MacInnes, in a novel written at the time, tells of an incident in which a young West Indian man is running up the down escalator at a London underground station. He finally reaches the top and presents himself at the ticket barrier. The white ticket collector who has been glumly watching his performance takes his ticket and says 'You people are as mad as march hares'. 'We believe in fun, man', responds the black youth. 'Well we believe in peace and quiet', snaps the disgruntled Englishman.

The desire for 'peace and quiet' and 'keeping ourselves to ourselves' seemed hostile and unfriendly to the warm immigrants. They soon realized that they had arrived in a cold climate. One woman from Barbados described how, during her first winter in this country, she looked out of the window 'and I see this thing coming down . . . I thought it was Lux soap. And I stood there for hours.' Forty years on and the snow is well known to Britain's Afro-Caribbean community and for many, life in Britain is still life within a cold and hostile climate.

White British people may, from their particular standpoints, have a very clear view of themselves and of British society as free of racial prejudice, but a game we have sometimes played in racially mixed groups reveals a different picture. In this game everyone present, black people and white people, makes a list of occasions when they have witnessed a racist incident in Britain. The white people always scratch their heads and struggle to make a list at all, whilst the black people scribble furiously and need extra time to complete very long lists. We must all struggle to look through the eyes of our neighbours, black or white, and to strive to look in new directions towards other views.

In London we used to meet regularly with a group of black Christians worshipping in many different parishes. As we ate and drank and talked the same kind of stories kept emerging. We were told about the previously cold climate in English churches ('We came to expect racism from lay people, but we didn't expect it from the vicar'). We heard stories about children under-achieving at school, stories about suspicion of the police, and stories about the fear of living in a high-rise flat on dark nights.

After some months we realized that these stories (coming from senior and respectable church members) should really be heard by people holding responsibility in society and so we began to invite one or two of them along. Perhaps the most dramatic meeting was when the Area Commissioner of Police sat and listened to the story of the Afro-Caribbean woman who, living alone in a high-rise flat, was sleeping soundly in the middle of the night. Suddenly her front door was broken down and a group of armed police in riot gear crashed in and hustled her into the corridor as they searched her flat. Whilst she was still shaking with fear the radio of the officer holding her crackled. He listened, took off his helmet, smiled, put his hand on her shoulder and said 'Sorry love, we've got the wrong flat'. 'In a moment', she told us, 'he changed from being a monster from Mars, to being a friendly neighbourhood policeman.' 'But', she went on, 'I can't now help but be frightened of the police.'

The senior policeman listened to this and then shared some of his own story of how he often went home at night and wept over some of the painful incidents which occur on London streets and in London homes. He told of how those same streets are necessarily patrolled by young officers coming from all over the country, who, although having the best training which can be given, are not naturally 'street wise' and are often frightened by what they might find around the next corner. He said that standard police work depends a great deal upon information being provided by members of the public, and so if a section of the public is reluctant to provide information through suspicion or fear, mistakes are more likely to be made by the police in which innocent people suffer, which intensifies the spiral of mistrust.

Nothing was solved that night. But just being in the same room and listening to one another's experiences broke down a little the web of suspicion which we all have for those different from ourselves. The fear of the stranger, or of somebody different, lurks very near the surface of most societies. In the 1950s, an astonishing project was undertaken by a primary school teacher in a rural American town. She divided her class of all white children into those having blue eyes and those having eyes of a different colour (predominantly brown). She told the class that it had been discovered that blue-eyed children were brighter, better behaved, and cleaner than those having a different eye colour. The class believed her and within a week clear evidence appeared. The blue-eyed children sat together, began to look smarter, and performed better in class. In the playground fights started between the blue-eyed and the rest.

The following Monday she gathered the class together and told them that she had misread the discovery. In fact, blue-eyed children were worse than other children in every way, and the other children would do well to treat them with suspicion. Again the children believed her, and again the evidence appeared. The work of the blue-eyed children deteriorated, whilst that of the other children improved. Within a few days, a formerly bouncy and confident group of blue-eyed children became sullen and resentful.

When we first saw the film of this project we were shocked but told ourselves 'Well, children are susceptible', but the same teacher then conducted the same project with groups of adults (prison officers) with similar results. It seems that most human beings are very ready indeed to believe those who tell them that they are superior or inferior to others because of some difference in eye or skin colour, some difference in language or accent, or some difference in religion or belief. Meeting our neighbour in natural and normal ways is the most powerful antidote to those who would have us suspect, mistrust, or even hate our neighbour because of some of these differences.

Fortunately it is now almost impossible for aware Christians to regard those of other faiths as the heathen in their blindness bowing down to wood and stone in strange and distant parts of the world. Our next-door neighbours in Britain might well be practising members of a world faith other than the Christian faith, people of obvious godliness, compassion, and community concern, people often providing an opportunity for normally insular British people to have global links and understandings. The opportunity for the study of world faiths is now accessible in Britain in a way that was quite impossible for previous generations. Most school syllabuses include the major world faiths, and there are many adult opportunities for encounters with people of other faiths, and for visits to places of worship and community.

Our own experience is that if we enter into encounter and dialogue with people of other faiths we may realize that God is there and that his love is shown both in the people of other faiths and in the encounter itself. It is often sad to realize that many Christians who oppose inter-faith encounter and dialogue have no experience of it and may be looking in the wrong direction, towards themselves, and asking the wrong questions, namely 'How does this affect us and how do we defend our faith?', rather than expecting faith to be strengthened and expanded. True, it is not possible fully to appreciate a faith, including Christianity, without entering it, and thereby having the 'eye of faith'. Christians may however look away from themselves and may then see what God is doing through the people of other faiths, and through this learn more about and respect the spiritual journey of their neighbour. Indeed this encounter with those of other faiths can be a 'mirror' which teaches us more about our own spiritual journey by illuminating it in a fresh way, and in so doing strengthening and deepening our approach to God through Jesus Christ in the power of the Holy Spirit.

British people have not only a special opportunity to learn from and have dialogue with people of other faiths, but, perhaps more importantly, a special responsibility to do so, in loving their neighbours and as pioneers in a world where such freedom is rare. People who come to Britain from restricted and even dangerous situations are often grateful for opportunities to participate in inter-faith dialogue in Britain. One of our Christian visitors from a Far Eastern country, where inter-faith encounters are dangerous, illustrated this when he requested an extended visit to Southall to meet Sikh, Hindu and Muslim people and to visit their places of worship. He allowed himself to go to a new place, to meet new friends and to have new horizons in ways which would not have been possible to him at home.

Ease of transport brings visitors to Britain and also takes people from the West to be with people in other places on earth and in other cultures. Many people travel as a normal part of their work as well as for holidays and the increasingly popular educational visits. Whatever reason the traveller has to venture into new places she may be enriched by a new horizon or she may see everything through the glass windows of the hotel, car or coach, a mist of unimaginable shapes which may never make any sense. The Thai beaches are divided into 'those that incarcerate the Vietnamese . . .

and those that are playgrounds for tourists who tumble frivolously out of their jumbo jets'. The tourist who stays safely by the hotel pool will have the same horizon he had at home. The explorer who ventures beyond the film set of the tourist world will see things very differently and may never be the same again. We stayed with a family in Barbados where the mother worked in one of the big beach hotels. She was a devout member of the Anglican Church and she read the Bible and prayed every evening, and her prayers included the British and American tourists. Listening to her tell horror stories about some of the tourists' behaviour and clothing helped us to see our own country and some of its people with new eyes, and made us realize that it is possible to travel half the way around the world as a tourist to visit new places, and yet never 'be there' at all!

Being there

Jesus of Nazareth's power as a simple presence lay in what he was, a person of God. The Church through the ages and today may have the power of simple presence if it is of God. One of the advantages of the Church of England is that it works from a parochial rather than a congregational model, so that every inch of the country is in a parish and has a church and priest to relate to. Churches have traditionally been built on hills and in other prominent places and during our 1991 visit to the diocese of Zanzibar and Tanga our group of Kenyan and British people dug the foundations for a new church on a hill, overlooking a huge sisal estate.

The group lived in a youth centre in Korogwe and was woken up every morning to the sound of the church bell ringing and resounding round the local hills to announce the morning Eucharist. The Archbishop of Tanzania, John Ramadhani, had brought the bell from England to act as a reminder to the people in the Usambara Hills that the church was there for them. The visiting group had until then taken church bells for granted. John Ramadhani came from the island of Zanzibar, where the diocesan cathedral of Christ the King was deliberately built by Bishop Steere on the site of the former slave market. The cathedral is entered where the former slaves entered the market. The slaves were piled up on platforms, like bags of rice, to test their resilience, and those who died were thrown into the ocean. Those who survived were taken to the marketing place, where they were whipped to test whether they would be suitable for hard work, and then auctioned. Any children who were too weak to work were slaughtered and their blood was drained through a tunnel into the sea. The high altar of the cathedral stands where the auctions took place. The font has been positioned on top of the tunnel and the baptismal water drains away through the same tunnel which once drained away the children's blood. The cathedral, completed in 1880, made a major contribution to the life of the surrounding community simply by being built; it was a sign of hope in a place of despair and confusion.

Perhaps in modern Britain we do not have such dramatic symbolic places (but it is interesting to remember that one reason why Christian missionaries were sent to Britain was because English slaves were seen in the slave markets in Rome), but our church buildings still proclaim the Church's presence by simply 'being there'. There is a cathedral or parish church on a hill, reminding our community of its history and roots. There is a re-ordered church in the market place, opening its doors as drop-in centre, community forum, or exhibition centre. There is the inner-city Victorian building, home to a Church community, small but lovingly hopeful in the uncertainties and confusions of urban living. There is the suburban modern building, perhaps the only shared building in a sea of houses, where the new inhabitants can come out of their privacy and discover the joy of being with others and creating community. But our buildings are of limited effect unless we the people in them develop the same style of 'being there'.

A Methodist friend went to work in the Solomon Islands as an engineer and was a little surprised when the bishop told him that his value in the islands as a person and his day-to-day living with the people were far more significant than his engineering work could ever be.

We went to Calcutta with a group from Britain and Germany and when we landed at the airport we were met by our hosts, a multi-faith community of young men and women committed to working with the people of the city at grassroots level, in primary health care, primary education and community development. We were taken on a hair-raising taxi journey through the city and straight to a slum area to meet the community, and to see the craft exhibition they had mounted. When we entered the community meeting room we quickly noticed a huge chart on the wall entitled 'How to increase your weight'. We had arrived in an unfamiliar milieu. We will always remember the warm hospitality we received in that needy place from people who obviously had very few material possessions, and we will always remember our astonishment when the community leader came to speak to us.

He explained that the communities of Calcutta had lived through many years of experts visiting them and telling them what to do, even giving them money and getting them started on development projects. The day always came, however, when the experts went away, and the local people became frozen by their own feelings of comparative inadequacy, and by their material poverty and perpetual listlessness due to a meagre diet and persistent ill health. Our host challenged us to be content to be in Calcutta as guests, appreciating the wonderful opportunity we had to meet the people, to visit their homes, to listen to their stories and to share their ideas for their futures. He said that our simply being there, with the people, in their homes and on their terms, was in fact a gift in itself, because it would give them a window on to the world and an experience of being valued as they were. He hoped then that a new energy for creating ideas for community development and for putting them into practice would arise from the people themselves. He went on to say that our presence might also be a gift for us and our own home communities if we were prepared to listen and learn. 'My people have wisdom for you, you know', he said, 'Help is not all one way.'

We had heard that message before, because it was the central theme of *Faith in the City*, the report of the Archbishop of Canterbury's Commissioners examining life and mission in Britain's inner cities. The report was different in style and content from most Church reports because first of all the authors made the effort to 'be there'. In small groups they went and shared the lives of those living in the decay of inner-city tenements, or the high-rise flats, or the forgotten outer council housing estates. Perhaps because of this the report spoke with real authority when it made it clear that for Church and community development to be effective and long-lasting it must be 'local, outward looking, participatory'. Only the local people themselves can make such work local, but we can all participate in one another's mission by 'being there', and through being there we help to open one another's eyes and hearts.

Being there actively

The simple presence of the people of God is no passive thing, but an active presence, a waiting, an accumulation of experience and skill so that when action is ultimately taken, it is effective action. T. S. Eliot in his poem *East Coker* alludes to this waiting.

I said to my soul, be still, and wait without hope
For hope would be hope for the wrong thing; wait without love
For love would be love of the wrong thing; there is yet faith
But the faith and the love and the hope are all in the waiting.

The athlete knows the style well. Months of preparation precede perhaps a few brief moments of performance. The golfer Tony Jacklin once wrote that when he
played a poor shot in a match he would return home and
practise that shot until he could play it perfectly. Then
when he was faced with the shot in another match it was
as though, he said, he was in a 'cocoon of concentration'—everything was shut out until the shot had been
played.

Perhaps that kind of concentration lay behind the gospel
story of Martha and Mary. Martha, naturally flustered when
a group of friends and neighbours unexpectedly called and
wanting to put on a good domestic show, was distressed to
find that her sister Mary was sitting like one of the guests,
listening to Jesus. 'Tell her to help me', she asked Jesus.
Jesus refused: 'Mary has chosen the good, and it won't be
taken from her.' Mary had chosen the good of an active
waiting on God. The time for Mary to act would come—she
was one of the few disciples prepared to wait by Jesus' cross,
but now was the time of waiting, of 'being there' with
Jesus, in the corner of her own sitting room.

Westerners do not always have the patience of those of
other cultures, however. We were once driving a Sri Lankan
friend back to London from a meeting in Oxford late at
night, thinking about the need to be in bed in time to get
enough sleep to work the next day, when the car broke
down. We were jumping around anxiously, and rushing to
ring up the AA and prowling up and down, when our
friend asked 'Why are you worried? Why can't you enjoy
the peace and quiet on this road, which we would never
have known if the car had not broken down?' We tend to be

so dominated by our plans that we never live in the present or appreciate it.

Sometimes the 'just being there' is forced upon us, but it can still be a creative time waiting on God and God's future. Nelson Mandela was imprisoned for twenty-five years, but not a moment seemed lost or wasted. Even when he was in solitary confinement he remained a sign of the suffering black majority of South Africa; then with his colleagues gradually a 'government in waiting' was formed, so that on their release negotiations with the ruling party could immediately be commenced.

There surely is no more naturally active person than Terry Waite, who travelled the world on the staff of the previous Archbishop of Canterbury, and who was best known by the public for his work in seeking to enable hostages to be released. No wonder so many people were anxious when he himself became a hostage. How would such a big, active man cope with enforced idleness? What would he be like if and when he was released? To our joy, it was the same old Terry Waite who came back to his family and friends. He had survived for several years with just a Bible and his own thoughts for company. But even in the darkest days, he related when he returned, he had been determined that nothing would be wasted, that it would all be used for good.

Sometimes in the midst of our active waiting, we are surprised by the thought of who we are, or what we might become. There is the Hindu story of the tiger cub brought up with a flock of sheep, so that it grew to behave like a sheep and to eat grass. One day a tiger strayed into the flock and the sheep scattered, but the tiger cub was asleep and the tiger caught it, surprised to find that it was a tiger. The tiger cub would not believe that it was anything but a sheep, so the tiger took it to a pond and forced it to look at its reflection in the water, challenging it to behave like a tiger and not like a sheep, challenging it to become what it

already was, to be itself. To become what we are we first
have to like ourselves, and to enable others to become what
they are, different, and equally precious to God, we have to
like and respect them. If people are disliked they normally
lose confidence and become depressed and inactive, and if
people are hated their depression is worse. Sometimes
hatred, on a personal, institutional or political level,
becomes a vicious circle, so that those who are despised
feel rejected and inadequate and express their anger by
despising and persecuting others. All the more reason why
Christ's mission must include the struggle to love and
accept other people as they are, and not as we would like
them to be.

Being there gladly

If we find it hard to love and accept other people as they
are perhaps we should ask ourselves whether we are in the
right place in being with them at all. In the last decade of
the twentieth century perhaps we need to move beyond
the typical Victorian missionary who thought he was
'slumming', whether at home or overseas, making great
sacrifices for the poor people he worked with. This type of
mission, if it can be called mission at all, is surely worse than
staying at home, for it leads to the bitterness of those who
think they have made all the sacrifices and of those who feel
perhaps that they have been done good to when they would
far rather have been left alone.

Fortunately, throughout the history of the Church, many
people have gone forth gladly, fully realizing their privilege
and their opportunity for themselves learning and changing. We ourselves went to live in Zambia partly because the
Anglican Church there wanted a Christian presence and
chaplain at the university, which had been established in
Lusaka as a secular institution soon after the country

achieved its independence from the British. We also went because we wanted the experience of living in Africa. In our five years in Africa we certainly learnt much more than we taught in either electronics or modern history. We learnt about tropical farming, about fruits, flowers and trees, about strange animals and crops. We learnt about new ways of building homes and of living together in the family and in the community. We travelled to mission stations all over the country, to game parks and to the famous and beautiful Mosi O'Tunya (Victoria Falls). Most importantly of all we met new friends and in our sharing with them we saw the world with new eyes. One year the Zambian government declared that Christmas Day would be a normal working day, and the Christmas Eucharist for the university students had to be held very early in the morning, before the teaching day began. We had a glimpse of the lives many Christians have lived, and live now, as small and unconsidered minorities.

When we lived in Zambia our Zambian friends and students expected us to behave culturally as if we were in England, and for much of the time we did, living in a Western-style house on the edge of the university campus. It was the few times when we were able to cross over which were the exciting and creative times, when we were invited to homes, to eat locally produced foods cooked in the traditional way, and when, on our travels, we were able to see traditional ways and wisdoms at work. When we went on a history field trip to Livingstone the students naturally expected us to stay culturally at home in the European style hotel but they were delighted when we camped with them and ate the traditional *nshima* (maize meal and water). They were only happy, however, because we actually preferred to camp, and we got to know them then as people, with parents and children, with fears, hopes and dreams. Our time in Zambia in the early 1970s could never have been called a sacrifice. It was a time of sharing and of learning and it made a difference to our lives, and to our work on our return to Britain.

The Christian presence can only have a value if it is chosen or accepted gladly. The inner-city priest who talks of nothing but his security alarm system cannot be as accepted or as useful as the one who keeps open house and enjoys visiting the high-rise flats and his parishioners even if they are in far away hospitals, hostels or prisons. One of these priests, well known to us, has such a valuable ministry walking the streets and catwalks, and even in the most tense times being alongside youngsters in distant borstals whose own parents have neither the desire nor opportunity to make regular visits. The Trustees of the Church Urban Fund have had the sense to see what a valuable ministry this is for the local community and have provided the funds for a parish administrator to keep the 'parish shop open' for the local congregation when their vicar is engaged elsewhere.

Most urban clergy, it seems, like to be where they are and intend to stay there. One of the encouraging findings of the Gallup Poll which accompanied the *Faith in the City* report was that a greater proportion of inner-city clergy were more positive about their ministry than clergy in any other environment. Whilst they might have considered moving, they usually wanted to move to a similar sort of parish.

Of course this does not mean that these clergy are particularly skilled or dedicated, but it does mean that they, often with their families, share the trials and tribulations, the joys and opportunities of their neighbours. This surely is one of the Church of England's major contributions to national life: the clergy, unlike every other professional group of people, live where they work and show up in the difficult as well as the comfortable corners of the land. It was the ability to say to politicians of all parties and people of good will 'Come and see; share our life for a few days' which gave *Faith in the City* its authority. Personal presence was everything.

We have had a taste of the challenges and joys of such living ourselves. We spent eleven years in the diocese of London. For the first five years we lived in Harrow where we brought up our family happily in a typical corner of 'comfortable Britain'. Then the work changed and we moved four or five miles nearer the centre of London to Kilburn in the borough of Brent. In making the move we crossed the invisible boundary between 'comfortable' and 'uncomfortable' Britain just at a time when boroughs such as Brent were facing a financial crisis and the local politicians and administrators were heroically trying to keep a skeleton of public services going against all the odds.

The move was a shock. Of course we rejoiced in the vibrant, multi-cultural life of Kilburn, even when we discovered that we had to empty our own dustbins or risk increasing the number of rats in the neighbourhood. A child became ill and we discovered that it was not as easy as in Harrow to book an appointment with the doctor on the corner; it meant queueing in a waiting room crowded to overflowing (but at least a doctor was prepared to take us as patients; had we been living in a bed-and-breakfast hotel, the accident unit at the hospital would have been the place for us). Obtaining a ticket to travel on the Underground could take up to twenty minutes as the machines were broken more often than not. (This situation would not have been tolerated in Harrow, but if you meet with frustration in every area of life you soon become passive and lethargic, or very, very angry.) None of this of course should have surprised us because such situations were spelled out in the pages of *Faith in the City*, but there is nothing like personal experience for making a situation real, and a touch of reality does no harm to our faith.

Being there with God

Being there on other people's territory can be very difficult, for it means moving from where we are to be where others are, in their place, in their situation and on their terms. It means making the greatest human effort to cross over to the other, to cross over to a way of life we find strange, physically, mentally and even spiritually, to stand where others stand and to look in the direction they are looking in. When we do this we discover that God is there, 'the light lighting every person'.

When E. M. Forster was travelling in India he visited Hindu temples, but he didn't like them and was tempted to write off the whole of Hindu culture because to him, with his cultural background, the temples were ugly and of glaringly bad taste. But then he realized that he was looking at Hinduism in the wrong way. He realized that he could only see what was beautiful and of God when he looked at the expressions of devotion on the faces of the people. How wrong he had been to judge the temples and even the Hindu religion with his own religious and cultural spectacles. How often we look in the wrong places and make quick and easy judgements of other people's ways of life and wisdoms.

We took a group of Kenyan Christians to Southall, to meet a variety of the people living there, including Christians, Sikhs, Hindus and Muslims. The Kenyan Christians had to be persuaded to meet the people of other faiths and could at first see no point in doing so. Finally, after long discussions, they reluctantly agreed to go to the Sikh gurdwara and to have lunch with the people there, as their guests. We felt tense and anxious as we went to meet the community leaders and to thank them for having us all, when behind us we heard loud laughter and we turned to see a group of Kenyan visitors and local Sikhs laughing and talking together in Swahili, for the Sikhs had come to

Southall from Uganda. The Kenyans were so happy to be able to speak in Swahili that all the barriers were at once broken down and sharing and learning followed. When the next year we took a British group to Kenya, the youth leader told everyone the story of the visit to Southall, and of the Kenyan Christians' mistaken judgement of the Sikhs as 'bad' and of their discovery that they were 'good people'.

When we go with groups to Kenya we arrange for them to take part in work camps, travel around with the Kenyan hosts and stay in families. When we stayed in one Kenyan family we noticed that the mother of the family, who had four children and was also a teacher, seemed to be doing practically everything about the home and on the small farm. She fed and milked the cows and goats, she kept hens and ducks, and she grew a fine range of crops, including maize, sugar cane, arrowroot, coffee and many fruits. She gathered and cooked the food, and cared for the children and the elderly relative who lived with them. We thought that she was obviously oppressed, and suggested that next time a Kenyan group came to England on an exchange visit she should come instead of her husband, and he could stay at home and do all the work and care for the children. She paused for a moment and then said 'I will come one day, perhaps when the children are older, but now when he goes away we just carry on, but if I were to go away he could not manage'. We had looked through our own cultural spectacles and so had mistaken her strength for weakness.

Being there without judgement requires us to be there with other people without trying ourselves to change anything, recognizing that if change is to be made it is the local people themselves who must do it because they wish to do it. This listening and enabling work is very difficult indeed, because it is natural for most people to think that the way they do things is the most sensible way. It is not only Westerners who think that they know best. When a British and Kikuyu group visited a Maasai manyatta (homestead) in the semi-desert area of northern Kenya, the Kikuyu members of the group were quite clear. They looked at the nomadic Maasai and said that their way of life would obviously be improved if only they would cease to be nomads and would instead plough up some of the land, grow food and become farmers. It was difficult for people who love farming like the Kikuyu to appreciate that the Maasai do not, and that they are nomads because moving about with their cattle is their traditional way of living and of relating to the world, and is also the way they have come to experience God.

The 1991 World Council of Churches Assembly took place in Canberra, the capital of Australia, and so Aboriginal affairs featured high on the agenda. During one of the weekends we took the opportunity to travel around a little and to meet some of the Aboriginal leaders nearer their home territory. One of them told us of the confusion being experienced by her people. A mining corporation had been given the right some years ago to mine for bauxite on her people's traditional homeland. The company had approached the task in what they believed to be a humane and enlightened manner. The Aboriginal people had been compelled to move temporarily from their homeland to a neighbouring piece of land where houses, clinics, schools and training places had been established. Meanwhile the company had ripped off the topsoil of their land and mined the bauxite, and had put the topsoil back again. The company was now encouraging the people to return to their traditional land and could not see that it was not the same land. In Aboriginal culture, the stories which make up the tradition of the people are associated with particular bushes and rocks and rivers. Those features of the landscape had disappeared and so the traditional stories no longer fitted. The land was now as strange to them as if they had landed on the moon. They had to begin to inhabit it anew as from the dawn of time.

Perhaps we would live more creative lives if we approached

our global village in that way—as being a strange and wonder-filled place, yet a place where our stories and traditions no longer quite fit. A place where we have to 'be' for a while before we can do or witness, or our doing may be the wrong kind of doing, and our witness the wrong kind of witness.

Ideas and resources

Ideas

- Members of a group may share their own resources, including poetry, pictures, music etc. to illustrate the uniqueness and value of every person and the possibility of every person using his or her gifts and resources for others.
- Share in a group or reflect on experiences you have had of meeting people with a different language, culture or way of life from your own. What did these experiences make you think?
- In what way is your local church a 'symbolic place'? Discover something of its history and its significance to the local community.
- Offer hospitality to people from a variety of backgrounds and cultures in your church and community. Find out about the places they come from. Learn to cook their food.
- Visit places of worship and community of people of other faiths in your local area or in a neighbouring area. Make time to get to know people of other faiths and to develop friendship and trust.
- Set up an opportunity to listen to refugees and others who are new to your community.

Group Bible study

Read Luke 10.38–42.

Read the story of Jesus' visit to Martha and Mary and allow time for quiet reflection.

- Act out the story in the group.
- Share how you would have felt if you had been Martha.
- Share a time or times when you have been upset over all the work you had to do.
- Discuss your views of why Jesus supported Mary in her listening role.
- Make individual lists of the challenge of the story for members

of the group and for particular people in the community. Share the lists and resolve to make at least one change, either as a group or individually.

Resources

For the addresses of your neighbours of other faiths and for people in local inter-faith groups contact:
Interfaith Network,
5–7 Tavistock Place,
London WC1H 9SS

Christians Aware will help you to contact people from overseas, including students and refugees:
Christians Aware,
10 Springfield Road,
Leicester LE2 3BD

The Commonwealth Institute can be visited for information on Commonwealth countries:
The Commonwealth Institute,
230 Kensington High Street,
London W8 6NQ

Suggested reading

What Lies Ahead? Listening to Refugees (Christians Aware, 1992).
Kosuke Koyama, *Three Mile an Hour God* (SCM Press, 1979).
Timothy Biles, *Windows on the Sudan* (Creeds, 1991).
Michael Nazir-Ali, *From Everywhere to Everywhere* (Collins Flame, 1990).

Brave witness

Mr Khrushchev, when he was general secretary of the Communist party in the Soviet Union, was once addressing a gathering of party officials. After his talk a voice called out from the back 'What were you doing when Stalin was carrying out his purges?' Khrushchev said 'Will the man who asked that question please stand up, and then I'll answer him'. Nobody moved. 'Yes', said Khrushchev, 'and that's exactly what I was doing—keeping my head down.'

President Bush recently addressed the Polish Parliament in Warsaw. He promised them 100 million dollars to give a boost to Polish businesses, they wished him long life of a hundred years. The remarkable developments during the last few years in Poland through the efforts of members of the Church and of the Solidarity movement are a reminder to us that people don't always keep their heads down even in difficult and dangerous times, and that when they have the courage to speak out, occasionally they trigger off an avalanche of public opinion. Few of us have that sort of courage, but even the most cautious of us have moments when we feel that we have to witness to our deepest hopes and dreams.

Some 20 years ago I was teaching electronics in the engineering department of the University of Zambia. As a priest I also acted as chaplain and was on the staff of the cathedral. The Zambian government had entered into technical agreements with several nations and our staff in the department of engineering included three British, two Americans, and six academics from the Soviet Union. As colleagues we worked together well enough. But this was still in the days of the Cold War, and it was obvious that each of the lecturers from the Soviet Union had been hand-picked as being ideologically sound.

Christmas came around and I was celebrating midnight Communion in the cathedral. As I gave the worshippers their communion I suddenly found myself offering the cup to one of my Russian colleagues. His eyes gazed into mine, and we shared a glance of fear and wonder before I passed on to his neighbour. There's no doubt, that in those dark days, if the party had known of his presence in the cathedral that night, he would have been flown back home the next week and would never have been *allowed out again. What was it in the faith of that man which had caused him to risk career and safety in an act of public commitment even if it was known to himself and God alone?*

Thankfully, we now live in more hopeful times, but I often reflect upon that brief incident. My colleague was no great hero, but he plucked up enough courage to make a small public act which reminded him of what he truly believed. Such small acts create the climate which enable the heroic acts to be effective. Let's not despise them. Following conscience is often a lot better than following crowds.

Section Two

Just Action

William Morris wrote a poem 'Love is enough'. A reviewer simply wrote 'It isn't'. Christians use the word 'love' a great deal, and 'to love your neighbour as yourself' is a teaching near the heart of most world religions. This approach to discipleship is sometimes the best, usually when we are considering the needs of our immediate neighbour or an obvious emergency. It is generally less adequate when we begin to consider the needs of distant neighbours or the relationships between human groups rather than between individuals. Then we need to translate the demands of love into the demands of justice. Then we must not only send our five pounds to charity but go on to ask ourselves both where the five pounds came from and why it is needed. We should not, however, stop sending the five pounds. At present for every ten pounds we spend, we give on average six pence to charity. There is no danger that we are about to overwhelm the world with our generosity of giving.

We need to show both kindness of heart and kindness of head. Kindness of heart leads us to take immediate action to meet human need. Speaking at the February 1992 General Synod of the Anglican Church, Terry Waite said that he returned to Beirut in 1987 notwithstanding the warnings that he might be taken prisoner because '. . . when the Church makes a commitment to people in trouble, the

Church does not walk away'. Kindness of heart is a basic Christian instinct, kindness of head goes further, to examine every aspect of an issue or situation, including the long-term possibilities of various responses. It prompts us to ask 'What is causing this state of affairs, and what can be done to change it?' In situations of injustice it asks questions not only about the sharing of wealth, but also about the sharing of power. In this section we will consider our Christian calling to compassionate service; to thoughtful development; to social prophecy; to be the pioneering people of God.

'The ultimate most holy form of theory is action. Not to look on passively while the spark leaps from generation to generation, but to leap and burn with it.' So wrote Nikos Kazantzakis in *The Saviours of God*. The Christian is a life-bringer, a transmitter of life, called to share in Jesus Christ's kingdom calling to bring 'Good News to the poor, release to the captives . . . to remove the chains of oppression and the yoke of injustice, to let the oppressed go free, to share with the hungry, and give homes to the homeless poor, to give clothes to those who have nothing to wear'. Christianity must be as much about the kingdom as about the Church. We must constantly remind ourselves that our faith has as much to do with human growth for justice and development as it has to do with Church growth and development. Our task includes both the relief of suffering and the looking towards the kingdom of God—the kingdom of community, justice, peace and love—globally and locally, not merely dreaming about what might be, but working under God for what might be.

First aid: Compassion

A cynic wrote about a particularly worthy person 'He's a great do-gooder, and you can tell the people he does good to by the hunted looks on their faces'. The Christian call to service is no mere do-goodery. The Gospel challenge is rather wider than Charles Kingsley's nineteenth-century challenge to 'Do the job that's nearest, tho' it's dull awhiles, helping where they need it, lame dogs over stiles'. Indeed we can only begin to do any good at all if we are prepared to receive as well as to give. The gospels make it clear that the Christian is a life-bringer for herself as well as for those with whom she is working. Doing good with others always brings blessing and pain to oneself. No matter how poor or struggling God's people are, and every person is poor or struggling in some way, there is always something to learn and something to receive. Cardinal Hume said at an inter-faith gathering in London that every person he meets is in some way his superior. If we could remember his words as we seek to do God's will in serving others there would be less chance of our actions being mis-understood or seeming patronizing.

Ronald Wynne spent years living and working among the Hambukushu people, refugees from Angola in North-ern Botswana, listening to their stories and learning their language, and from this rich experience he said 'Don't try to teach anyone anything until you have first learnt some-thing from them'.

The world-wide L'Arche communities have based their work with mentally disabled adults upon the firm belief that every person is a unique gift from God who has some-thing to give to others. The communities are created around all the people in them, and all, mentally disabled and others, contribute, by their work and by their special quali-ties, which are only revealed because each person is accepted as he or she is and therefore feels safe and relaxed. We have had the privilege of visiting L'Arche communities, and have spent days with the people, on pilgrimage and in worship and workshops. Like every visitor we discovered that we received much more than we gave.

Western people and rich and educated people everywhere have as much to learn from materially and physically poor and struggling people as they have to give. One of the consequences of the follow-up to *Faith in the City* has been the way in which those who live in 'comfortable Britain' have been enlightened and sometimes inspired by the wisdom, courage, and experience of those living in the less comfortable inner cities or estates. This should not surprise us for we are taught that our faith was born in a stable, was focused on a cross between thieves, and found its form in the teaching of a Messiah who was at home amongst the ordinary folk of his day, good and bad alike. The 'good news to the poor' is surely good news not only to the materially or physically poor, but also to the materially and physically rich, who may not, because of their condition, know their need of God, the greatest poverty of all.

It is sometimes said that compassion and service may be inappropriate responses to human suffering and struggle, because they can lead to feelings of power and control in the helpers and they can encourage the people helped to feel dependent and therefore less confident to do anything themselves. There is some truth in this. As we have written earlier, we were told in Calcutta that some of the relief and development workers there had immobilized local people and that simple presence and listening were much more useful than action.

It may also be true that help and relief given to people living under unjust regimes may merely keep people going and therefore prop up the regimes. Many people who are suffering under unjust systems say that they do not wish outsiders to offer them comfort. They would rather challenge outsiders to remove any props they may have offered to the unjust systems, and so hasten their collapse. This has always been the argument of supporters of democracy in South Africa who have encouraged economic sanctions by the world community against the minority government there. It seems clear that world-wide sanctions have prompted the South African business community to bring pressure for political change. Those who encourage first aid are often those who benefit from the regimes causing the suffering in the first place.

In many suffering situations around the world the help needed is an obvious matter of life and death, and even then a true human partnership is possible. In some situations people may prefer death to an undignified existence, and if we love them we must respect their choice. In other situations, when help is desperately needed, we may not be able to take time to listen and learn, as Ronald Wynne did in Botswana. However his attitude of respect and of awareness of God in the people may always be possible, even towards those we have only just met or heard about, and no matter how desperate they may be. In this way helpers may become partners in a creative relationship, rather than mere do-gooders.

When we were in Calcutta we were challenged by someone who is world famous for her compassion and loving service of the poor, and who has written

> When a life comes into my hands,
> all my love and my energy goes
> to support that life,
> to help that life to grow to its fullness,
> because that person has been created
> in the image of God.

(From *My Brother, My Sister*)

Mother Teresa's work is urgent because it is work with hungry babies and children and the destitute dying in Calcutta. She has taken her simple faith, that the Christian should love God and neighbour, very seriously indeed. She has simply, faithfully, generously, ungrudgingly and determinedly given her life to God and to poor people; and she has said that she is the receiver. The unlooked for result of her transparent singleheartedness has been that she has inspired hundreds of people to join her Missionaries of Charity, and thousands of people, in India and throughout the world, to feel challenged by her.

There is a story told that early in her ministry with the poor and dying she was visited by a well-wisher who watched her bathing the legs of an elderly sick pavement resident. 'I couldn't do your work for a million pounds', the visitor said. 'Neither could I', came the swift reply. The work of caring is not done for money, but for the love of the Christ whom Mother Teresa always sees in the faces of the poor and the dying.

We visited Shishu Bhavan in Calcutta, one of the children's homes run by the Missionaries of Charity, where the problems are enormous but where the children are loved and loving in their turn. We were told about the contentious feeding programmes for the poor, which are seen by the sisters as a temporary stop-gap, until the people have a way forward; and we went fearfully to Nirmal Hriday, Mother Teresa's home for dying destitutes, where we were surprised by the peacefulness of the place. The home is a stone-floored double hall, and the people lie in rows, huddled up under the dark blankets. The Indian sisters rush around constantly and whilst we were there people were brought in, a man died and a body was taken out.

Second aid: Recognizing the need

There are many thousands of needy people, in Britain and around the world, who desperately cry out for a Mother Teresa to love them, to learn from them and to help them in their suffering. In Britain alone there are the old, the chronically ill, the mentally ill and disabled, the prisoners, the lonely, the homeless, and countless others, all created in the image of God. It is not that people do not care about this abyss of human need, it is that we are afraid, and sometimes ambivalent in our response. As we pass the beggars and run-down estates on our way to our more comfortable homes we say both 'Don't you dare raise hard questions concerning all this with me' and 'Help me out of my guilt'. Our responses to God's people often make it clear that we are also the poor.

A story told of Queen Victoria is that when the royal train approached the Black Country in the Midlands on its way between London and the North-West, the queen would ask for the blinds to be drawn down 'because the view depressed her'. A similar story comes from the East where we are told that a certain sultan's servants would take him to the mosque by a roundabout route across the town to avoid the sight of the beggars in the slums; for the local tradition was that to see the plight of the needy and to do nothing to aid them 'turned the heart to stone'. The sultan's servants protected him from that fate by keeping his eyes away from need.

We in the West have more sophisticated ways of avoiding encounters with people in need. Those of us who live in cities have developed the art of never catching the eye of fellow travellers and frequently of not even knowing the name of our next-door neighbour, let alone his need. In our work in community development we have discovered that, apart from the clergy, virtually the only people who know the true situations of the people of their neighbourhoods are the postmen and milkmen, because they visit most houses on most days. Giving a party for postmen and listening to their stories taught us an enormous amount about our neighbourhood.

Another way of avoiding our neighbours' need is to

blame them for their condition. 'It's all very sad, but really it's all their own fault.' A game we have played with a variety of groups in Britain asks participants to make two lists of reasons for the poverty and suffering in so much of Africa. The first list should be of things the African people themselves are responsible for; the second of things the West is responsible for. In most cases the lists of mistakes made by the African people are long, and lists including the involvements and mistakes of the West are very short. No doubt the result would be the same if we focused on the plight of the homeless, the unemployed, the rootless in our own society.

Yet another way of avoiding seeing our neighbour's need is so to bombard ourselves with images of need on our TV screens that our brains soon suffer from 'compassion fatigue' and we take in no more. The compassion of nations of people can be massively aroused, as it has been by the Live Aid, Sports Aid and similar appeals, but we and the media are fickle and if one part of the world is being helped then another is inevitably being ignored.

When, soon after the Gulf War, the focus of the world's attention was on the Kurds, and money was being collected for them, people were starving in Somalia, being persecuted in Tibet and forgotten altogether in places like East Timor and the formerly famous Cambodia. William Taylor was working in Jordan when the Gulf War started, and was involved in receiving and finding food and shelter for the thousands of refugees, people from all over the world, who went to Jordan from Kuwait. We visited Jordan with a group just after the war started, when the first refugees were arriving and the people of Jordan were responding kindly and helpfully. Later, the influx of refugees became huge and unmanageable, and William remembers that then, when he worked on the Jordanian border with Iraq, people were desperate for food and water and depended on the journalists getting the stories out to the wider community and to the world. For a time the help came, but then the focus of interest moved away from Jordan, and a year after the end of the Gulf War the badly weakened country has faced the entry of thousands of Palestinians from Kuwait. With little press interest in Jordan, there has been little international help in the new crisis.

Compassion and loving service are necessary human responses to urgent or chronic need, and they are the particular response of Christians who are called to bring the qualities of the kingdom of God a little nearer, but they are only one way forward, and are very limited in their impact. However hard loving people may work with others, the impression they make will be small and weak in the face of what needs doing in our world.

Many of the refugees who went into Jordan from Kuwait during the Gulf War were cared for and many were repatriated, though sometimes to appalling situations. There are many thousands of refugees in many places in the world who suffer and die, and nothing is done. When Timothy Biles, an Anglican priest, travelled in North and eastern Africa towards the end of 1990 he visited many refugee camps, and one of them was an Ethiopian camp for 18,000 unaccompanied Sudanese children. The children were unaccompanied because their parents had been massacred in the western Sudan in 1987. Tim visited the ward for dying children, which he found sickeningly shocking. He asked 'Why don't we know about these things in England?'

Avoiding our neighbour's eye, blaming our neighbours for their own need and suffering, hiding in compassion fatigue, in all these ways we pull down the blinds because the view depresses us. Perhaps in terms of our own protection and short-term salvation we are wise to do so, because 'pulling up the blinds' can lead us into difficult and complicated situations from which we may never escape. We have recent experience of offering hospitality to a small number of refugees who have arrived in Britain from the Middle East, and we are aware that they are the tiny tip of a huge and growing iceberg of refugees and displaced people who, mostly through no fault of their own, have nowhere to go and whose needs are great. Many refugees have said to us that they are often desperate for kindness and for sympathetic people to listen to their stories. They are lonely, homesick, vulnerable and suffering from culture shock; and we, individually and as Western nations, cannot cope, and are tempted to escape by blaming the suffering people themselves. Elie Wiesel has written of refugees that 'they plunge into a world that was there before they were and which has no need of them. They arouse fear just as they themselves fear.' We are afraid.

During a period of famine and disease in the East End of London during the nineteenth century *The Times* had a leader which read 'There is nothing to blame for this. It is a result of nature's simplest laws.' Those words sound shocking and callous to us today when applied to our own capital city, but it is precisely the attitude that we still have to much of the poverty, disease and powerlessness around the globe. It is an attitude which springs from fear. It is still not an adequate answer, but finding a more feasible way forward leads us into stormy waters—the waters of development and campaigning.

Development challenges

When we lived in Zambia we were once visiting a mission station when our baby was taken ill. We took him to the clinic run by nursing Sisters. The illness was diagnosed as tonsilitis and antibiotics were given to him. As we were leaving the clinic an African mother brought in her baby. We stopped to chat and discovered that the baby, the same age as our own, was suffering from the same disease. The child, of course, was given the same medicine.

Three days later our baby seemed better but we returned to the clinic for him to be checked over. The sister confirmed that all was well. We asked her casually 'How is the other baby who was here?' 'I'm sorry to tell you that he's died' she said. 'Died. He can't have died. He was the same age. He had the same disease and you gave him the same medicine. Our child is better. How can it be that the other child is dead?' 'Haven't you heard of malnutrition?' the Sister asked us, 'Most African children are suffering from it, due to lack of adequate protein and vitamins in the diet. Your baby is basically healthy and soon throws off a germ when treated with good medicine but, because of malnutrition, African children are a prey to any disease, and even though we treat them as best we can, they often go down hill very rapidly.'

Of course we had heard of malnutrition. But until that tiny African neighbour grabbed our attention we had no idea of its devastating effect. From that moment on we found ourselves immersed in trying to help the newly formed Lusaka Nutrition Group, which planned to organize health clinics in the townships of Lusaka and the wider area. The clinics bought and imported cheap and nutritious high-protein food from far and near—dried fish from Tanzania, milk biscuits from Australia, nuts from West Africa. Money had to be raised for the basic costs. The paperwork of import permits was immense. Work parties had to be organized to pack the food into manageable portions for sale. Other people offered their services in the clinics in the townships. The work was never-ending as the new group moved into the minefield of community development and on, much later, to the founding of a small farm where people could go to try out new farming techniques. We should not have been surprised. Such work will always be never-ending.

A story is told of an outbreak of disease in Constantinople. The religious authorities announced that the reason was due to the impiety of the people of Constantinople and called for repentance. A local doctor wrote that whilst the people of Constantinople might well be impious, the thing that they most needed to repent about was the state of their drains because these were the cause of the disease. He was jailed for impiety! Basic development work is sometimes today regarded as somehow 'unspiritual' or less 'Christian' than preaching or Bible study. We do not agree. Jesus taught us to expect to meet him in a variety of ways, and one was in removing the need of our neighbour. Many of us were taught that the way to bring change is to enable individuals to be changed by Jesus Christ. Then they change other individuals who in turn change the world. We now believe that that is only one half of the equation. Winston Churchill once said 'Men make institutions; institutions make men'. If that is right, and we believe that it is, then both individuals and institutions need to be touched by God's transforming power.

Perhaps the best-known Christian teaching about the service of neighbour is the parable of the good Samaritan and we rightly praise the action of the Samaritan. But we might speculate about what would have happened if the Samaritan had turned up half an hour earlier when the mugging was about to occur. Would he have 'had a go' at risk of life and limb? Would he have raced for the police and found himself a witness in a trial with his schedule disrupted? Would he have raised a petition about the lack of security for travellers on the road to Jericho? It is always far less complicated just to bind up the wounds, pay the hospital and hotel bills and go on one's way.

It is interesting to reflect on the difference in attitude of

Church members to two consequences of *Faith in the City*: the creation of the Church Urban Fund, and the Committee for Black Anglican Concerns. People took little convincing that we needed a Church Urban Fund and it is now a major charity. The need to fund projects in the inner cities was obvious. Christians around the country dug deep into their pockets and the money came.

Many people were far less convinced about the creation of the Committee for Black Anglican Concerns. It had to be pointed out that opportunities in society were not equally available for our black fellow citizens. Average unemployment rates for blacks were twice those for whites. (32 per cent of 16–24-year-old black men in London were unemployed.) Black people were four times as likely to be homeless. Nor was the situation in the Church much better. Although large numbers of people from ethnic minorities were worshipping in Church of England congregations Sunday by Sunday, they were not to be found proportionately in any of the structures of the Church, nor were they offering themselves for ordination in proportional numbers.

But wasn't it reverse racism to take positive action to change the situation? Wasn't it better to leave things as they were and assume that the black presence would eventually 'trickle through' into every aspect of the Church's life. The answer was 'No' and the Committee was set up because many black people wanted it, to feed the wisdom of black Christians into the highest levels of the Church's life and to make sure their concerns stayed high on the agenda of the Church. It is perhaps helpful to think of the analogy of scaffolding. When radical transformation is taking place in a building scaffolding is often constructed to provide alternative ways of entering the various levels of the building. When the transformation is completed the scaffolding can be removed because it is no longer necessary. So it is with 'positive action'. When it is obvious that significant minority groups are not reaching parts of the life of any organization by normal ways and the organization needs their wisdom and participation it is necessary to erect alternative scaffolding to enable them to gain access. When the life of the organization has been transformed by their presence then the scaffolding can be removed.

Development work begins with the task of erecting scaffolding with people in every land, to enable them to gain access to the resources they need to play their part in developing their societies.

> Give a man a fish and you are helping him a little bit, for a very short while; teach him the art of fishing, and he can help himself all his life . . . but teach him to make his own fishing tackle and you have helped him to become not only self-supporting but also self-reliant and independent.
>
> (E. F. Schumacher)

Christians have a story of 'good development practice' from the gospels—the story of Jesus' encounter with Zacchaeus. Jesus in calling Zacchaeus down from his tree and inviting himself to his house found the way of enabling Zacchaeus to receive, to give, and to change without losing his basic human dignity.

This surely is the primary task of sharing in development. There are many ways of building a bridge, or a village or town, and there are many and varied opinions of the ideal bridge, village or town. So who decides whose opinions and priorities should be accepted and which models should be adopted? It is surely wrong for decisions about development to be taken by people who do not live in the place concerned, even if they give money; and this must be as true for governments as it is for missionary societies, aid agencies and individuals. When people are enabled by friendship or by training or by gifts of money to make their own decisions and to put their own ideas into practice their energy and commitment may deepen and spread to those around them. When people are patronized and told what to do it seems likely that they will feel inadequate. Institutional do-gooding can be as resented as individual do-gooding.

We were privileged to be invited by the diocese of Zanzibar and Tanga to join the local people in digging a channel from the hillside to the fish pond in the village at Lewa. The fish pond had been planned by the village people a year earlier and our visit with a group was the opportunity for them to revive their plans. By the time we arrived they had already dug the hole where the pond itself would be. It seemed a very long way from the mountainside to the site of the pond in the middle of the village. The channel would have to be dug for a long distance and under a road before entering the village. When we all started to dig we had no idea of completing the task, but people came and joined in, and soon the whole village was at work, including the women who prepared delicious meals. Spirits rose and the channel was dug quickly, mainly by the local people. The complicated crossing of the road was tackled successfully by a pipe being cemented into the ditch and covered over. On the last day of our time in Lewa some of us climbed the mountain overlooking the village. When we returned from an expedition which took far longer than we had expected the Lewa church bell was ringing in celebration of a week which had surprised us all. The celebration continued into a ceremony of cutting a way for the water to flow through into the pond, and into the speeches made in farewell. When we left the village the pond was filling up and the people were planning to put fish into it and to share their experiences with other people in other villages. Soon there will be so many fish in the Lewa pond that some will be taken to a new pond in another village.

We have been privileged to have had first-hand experience of a variety of excellent examples of fine development work in different parts of the world. The Young Men's Welfare Society in Calcutta is made up of representative young people who are brought up and who live in the city. They work in the slum communities with the people, and ideas and work are developed and executed there. The motto of the society is 'Strength in People', and to be faithful to this the members focus their attention on girls' education and health in a country where it is estimated that as much as 29 per cent of the time of a girl in the rural areas is spent in the collection of fuel, and a further 20 per cent in the carrying of water.

YMWS schools now have 1,600 pupils and there is increasing community and parental involvement so that the drop-out rate of pupils, normally a big problem in India, is low. YMWS has recently launched an ambitious venture in helping to improve schools in rural Bengal and in sharing the development of a rural extension programme with the local people in three clusters of six villages. The building of a rural training-cum-service centre is planned, and the local people have built two new roads and have begun the first phase of a water project. Health camps are run and focus especially on women learning to take control of their own health and the health of their families.

Few people would question the worth of thoughtful development projects such as these, but there is a narrow line between becoming involved in practical development and in enabling social change, and then we enter the world of prophecy and politics. We do not believe that it is necessary to apologize for this involvement. If a lunatic is driving a car out of control down a crowded street, it is the duty of the Christian not only to care for the victims and to repair the damage, but also to attempt to wrest the steering wheel out of the hands of the person misusing it, to point out that person's irresponsibility and the destructive possibilities of such a course being continued, and to take steps to prevent such behaviour in the future. In such a situation the sacrifice of involvement is great but at least most sensible people would recognize the need for it in the face of an obvious evil. The sacrifice of involvement must be much greater when an evil is not recognized and then the pioneering prophet or political activist may be seen as a threat and may be very lonely and vulnerable. The obvious paradigm of Jesus on the cross may not be very much comfort in such circumstances.

Social prophecy

Harold Macmillan in his visit to Southern Africa in the 1960s spoke of 'A wind of change blowing through Africa'. Bishop Trevor Huddleston had a little earlier, in 1956, promised 'Naught for your comfort', whilst apartheid lasted, in his best-selling and prophetic book of that name. More recently he said that he hoped that apartheid would be dead before he was. It has taken some thirty years for the wind of change to develop into the gale which is blowing through South Africa. Trevor Huddleston has constantly campaigned for South Africa to move towards change, freedom, equality and justice. In his late seventies he returned there; in suffering for past, present and future violence, in hope, but by no means certain hope, for a future democratic South Africa, and in fear that other changes sweeping the world would mask South Africa's final trauma.

It is not enough for those of us who live in Britain and the West to admire old campaigners for freedom and justice in South Africa like Trevor Huddleston, Nelson Mandela and many more, or for us to remember those who died in the cause of freedom like Steve Biko and Ruth First. It is easy to admire from afar, and helpful to act in solidarity to support movements for a South African democratic and multi-racial future, but it is not too difficult to do so from another country. It is much more difficult for us to point out and combat the present destruction and bleak prospects caused by racism, sexism or poverty in our own countries, localities, churches and homes, and especially if we have to go on doing it whilst being ignored or despised. Wherever we live in the world we, individually and as the Church, must obviously listen to others in other places than our own and learn from them. We may thus be enriched and enabled to seek to understand our own history and current situations and behaviour. We may also be empowered to go on to appreciate and extend what is good and, if we are open to a struggle, to point out likely future consequences of what is destructive at the same time as working for change towards greater justice ourselves.

Predicting the likely implications of behaviour for the future was usually included in the messages of the great Hebrew prophets to the people of their day, and it was always within the context of looking back. The prophets reminded their people of where they had come from and what they had traditionally stood for. The prophets spoke of God's presence in history with his people, establishing a covenant with them, and from that base exhorted them to behave as a covenanted people, responsible and just, so that their future would be a blessing and not a curse. God had liberated the people when they were powerless slaves in Eygpt. God had acted graciously to them and they were therefore to act graciously, particularly to the poor, the oppressed and the vulnerable, also God's people.

When the Jewish Passover is celebrated and the story of the ten plagues of Egypt is retold, the Jews deliberately spill ten drops of wine from their glasses to represent the tears which the Jewish people shed for the Egyptians. The Bible portrays the Egyptians as oppressors of the Jews, and in their turn as victims of the Hebrew liberation. The rabbis tried to prevent the Jews from celebrating the defeat of the Egyptians. They said 'The angels too, wished to praise the power of God. But God silenced them, saying: "The work of my hand [the Egyptian army] is drowning and shall you sing a song?" ' Chief Rabbi Jonathan Sacks has written,

> . . . which is how as a child I learnt the two fundamental principles of Passover. A people who were once slaves must never enslave others. And to have faith is not simply to believe that God is on your side. When God brings about a victory, he remains the God who suffers with the victims of that victory.
>
> (From *The World Might Weep*)

The Bible and the Jewish traditions taught that graciousness was not only to be shown in personal charity, it was to be reflected in the systems and structures of daily living. The fields and vines were only to be gone over once at harvest time—the crops and fruits remaining were to be left for the fatherless and the widows. The Jubilee principle of cancelling debts aimed to prevent the inevitable inequalities in society from growing ever wider. The prophets were wiser than they knew. There are not only good theological reasons for living justly and generously, there are good social reasons for doing so, because it is not possible to build a civilized society on inequality and greed.

It is easy for those of us who do not live in the Middle East to deplore the failure of the state of Israel to continue in the best traditions and teachings of the Jewish faith and to fear for the future. It may perhaps be more useful for us to see the small signs of hope in the history and faith traditions of all the people in the region, Jews, Christians and Muslims, to learn from what some of them do towards reconciliation and peace and to work with them, in the

Middle East and at home. We have caught sight of many seeds of hope when we have met people, of all faiths, speaking and working for the dignity and equality of all the people in the Middle East, regardless of race or religion. We have met young Israelis who long for peace, and we have seen demonstrations by the Women in Black, the brave Israeli women who wear black every Friday and stand in West Jerusalem to protest against the occupation. We have visited a community, formed in 1972 and situated on a hill overlooking the Vale of Ayalon, in an area with a history of struggle and war from the days of Joshua until 1948. The community, Neve Shalom/Wahat al-Salaam, aims to develop understanding and respect between Jews and Palestinians, by offering programmes of meeting and working together for every stage in life. The encounters are often traumatic for it is hard for a Jew to meet a Palestinian who supports the PLO and the Intifada, and it is hard for a Palestinian to meet a Jew who will one day go into the Israeli army. The hope is in the meeting and for the future, when understanding may grow. The fear is that the tiny seeds of hope may be crushed by the hardness of heart which is so obvious everywhere, and the dread that understanding may come too late. Canon Riah Abu Al Assal of Nazareth is afraid that the Arab Christians, who have lived and worshipped in the region since the early Church was formed, may disappear from the Middle East altogether as they go abroad in the face of the increasing social, cultural and economic deprivation at home. We met a young Palestinian woman who had gone to live in Canada with her husband and baby because, she said, 'I do not want my children to hate'.

A creative society cannot be built on inequality, greed and hate in the Middle East or in any country in the world, including Britain. When we lived in Kilburn, in northwest London, we had several burglaries. One occurred at lunch time when we were taking our dog for a walk. The local police officer came, looked at our house, shook his head and said 'Your only protection against burglars is to get a dog'. We pointed out that we had a dog. He look at our small dachshund and said 'That won't do. You need a big dog.' We explained that the size of the dog would not have made any difference as we were taking it for a walk at the time of the burglary. Without a flicker of a smile the officer replied 'You need two big dogs. One which you leave on guard at home, whilst you're taking the other for a walk.' His logic was impeccable, but we don't wish to live our lives in the company of two fierce large dogs because we fear our neighbour. We would rather work for the kind of society where social harmony made such protection unnecessary.

The pattern of prophecy developed in the Bible, of looking back and reminding a society of its roots, responsibilities and journey forwards, has elements which we need to recover. For example, we need to be reminded of Churchill's 'safety net'. He maintained that we should draw a line below which we would not allow persons to live and labour, yet above which they might compete with all their strength. He wanted to see free competition upwards, but he believed that we should decline to allow free competition downwards.

We live in times when most of the great ideologies have lost their appeal. Socialism spreads the illusion that politics can answer every human problem, and that the perfectibility of human beings can be brought about by political action. This false doctrine at best brings disillusionment and weakens self-reliance, at worst it destroys lives. Capitalism takes a coldly realistic view of how people are and of what they want, but it exploits some of the more basic and nasty human instincts, unless it is tempered by Churchill's safety net. Of course we need wealth creation as well as wealth distribution, but wealth creation is not the same as shuffling money around the stock exchange, and cuts often increase expenditure. Cutting out an alcohol dependence unit in Britain can mean an increased need for police and hospital services. Reducing the number of council houses available leads to increased expenditure on bed-and-breakfast accommodation and there is also the added problem of the degradation of the people who have to live there. Cost cutting often merely means that the cost is passed on to other services.

We should be guided by the parable of the man who, disturbed by the cost of hay, was teaching his horse to eat less. He cut down its hay ration progressively each day. He was just at the point of success, when the horse had been taught to eat nothing, when the wretched animal died!

Competition by itself is not enough to build a just and harmonious society. It might be a crucial human instinct but so is co-operation, and both are needed if a nation is both to hold together and to prosper. Sin affects both, turning competition into unbridled personal selfishness, and co-operation into restrictive practices against poorer people or nations. The division between good and evil does not lie between societies or groups; it runs through the middle of individual hearts and corporate systems.

We are not helped in our prophecy, which must include a search after social morality, by the fact that Christians are divided, not so much over the importance of morality but over where the focus of morality should lie. Many people hold passionate views about social morality—sexism, racism, peace and justice and Third World issues—but may be casual about personal morality.

Similarly some of those most vocal about personal sin, the breakdown of family life, pornography, abortion and the rest, are quite blind to the social sins of society. The influence of this group could be clearly seen during the last debate in the House of Lords on Sunday trading. Two-and-a-half benches were full of bishops. Perhaps the matter was of vital importance. But was it of so much more importance than Third World debt, the levels of unemployment, homelessness . . . where a more modest episcopal presence in the Lords is usually seen?

The fact is that both personal and social morality are the bonds which hold society together, and both are elements in what Jesus called 'the kingdom of heaven'. His mission was to open people's eyes to the fact that God was with them in a new way and to invite them, individually and corporately, to live new lives in response to God's presence. He called them to live as the pioneering people of God.

Pioneering people of God

President John Kennedy is remembered as a great American social reformer. In fact, when he died there were some ninety social reform bills collecting dust, with no movement in the Senate or in Congress. Lyndon Johnson, thrust into power in tragic circumstances, was not noted as a great social reformer, yet he got those bills through. A meeting which he had with a group of fellow senators may indicate why he was successful with this programme of social legislation. He told his colleagues that they had to give him their votes in supporting a particular piece of black civil rights legislation: 'I was brought up in the same way as you, and I like this as little as you do, but I tell you that they've read the constitution and are demanding their rights. We've got to change.'

President Johnson would not perhaps have regarded himself as a social pioneer, but the elements of what we want to call 'the pioneering people of God' were present in his brief speech. These are the elements of hearing the word of God, seeing God's judgements, and having a vision of the resurrection. The pioneering people of God are the people who see and hear where God is saying 'No' to present systems and structures. They are the people who have a glimpse of God's 'Yes' for the future, and put themselves at the disposal of this 'Yes'. They are no mere voices in the wilderness. Voices in the wilderness may be important, but they don't necessarily change the nature of the wilderness. Christians, if they are to be the pioneering people of God, must see themselves as belonging, yet not belonging in their world—natives of their place yet foreigners in it, often affirmers of its life, but occasionally critical of its ways.

An informal meeting between American and English bishops during the 1978 Lambeth Conference was responsible for a significant development for the life of the urban Church in Britain. The English bishops, all of whose dioceses included substantial urban areas, discovered that their American counterparts met regularly together to discuss urban issues. The English urban bishops began to do the same and their wives were soon members of the group. It was in this group that many of the plans for *Faith in the City* were made and after its publication in 1985 the urban bishops made a critical contribution to the challenges which the report was making to the nation.

In pioneering, sometimes the moment when action is taken is critical to its success. Such was the case here. In 1985 *Faith in the City* was published and by 1987 the follow-up was getting into its stride in the Church. The 'challenges to the nation' had met with a mixed response, however. The fact is that urban issues at that time were not high on the agenda of any political party. Then came the 1987 General Election. The urban bishops' group, which we had by then joined, published an open letter to all political parties stressing that urban issues must be addressed in the manifesto of any political party which expected serious attention.

This initiative did not make the urban bishops popular, but it received wide publicity and it did have the desired effect—to heighten awareness of urban issues; indeed it might well have been one of the reasons why on election night, Margaret Thatcher, newly confirmed in office, said live on television, 'We must do something about the inner cities'. Of course since that time, all parties have produced a wealth of urban initiatives. We might not agree about the wisdom of some of these, but nobody can now complain about urban issues being neglected!

The most effective illustration we know of the spirit and contribution of pioneering comes from a brief cartoon which was once shown on television. It portrayed a little man walking down the corridor of a modern office block. He came to a wall blocking the way. He pushed the wall and, finding it solid, he sat down on a conveniently placed chair to wait. Another man came along. He too pushed at the wall and then put down his briefcase, took off his hat and coat, walked back down the corridor, and then ran and threw himself at the wall. Nothing happened except that he collapsed. He picked himself up and repeated the exercise and this time a crack appeared in the wall. He picked himself up again and ran and threw himself at the wall once more. This time the wall collapsed—on top of the little man. The other man meanwhile had been calmly watching all this. He now got up and, seeing that his way was unblocked, he climbed over the rubble and went on down the corridor. After a brief time the rubble shook and the little man emerged. He dusted himself down, put on his hat and coat, picked up his briefcase, climbed over the rubble and made his way forward. We followed him, around one corner, two, and then another wall blocking the way, and the first little man sitting and waiting!

The Christian pioneer seeks to remove the obstacles which are blocking the way of individuals or communities who are working for change towards human development. The pioneer points to the blocks and encourages others to work with her to remove them. Failing this the pioneer is prepared to throw herself at the blocks on behalf of others. The supreme example of such pioneering of course is that of Jesus of Nazareth throwing himself at the sin, the pain, the unfulfilment of the world, and bringing that world down upon his shoulders in the pain-filled death of the cross. Through that sacrifice the way to God's kingdom was unblocked, and the world saw a new way forward towards change and growth in the joy and fulfilment of Easter.

If the Church is to be a people engaged in 'just action' then like the little man in the cartoon, we may from time to time emerge bruised from our service, development, prophecy and pioneering. This should neither surprise nor depress. There are great world religions where calm and peace is the desired end. Christianity is not amongst them. The centre of our faith is not neat harmony, but a cross where things askew are being renewed and transformed. Yet our just action is incomplete unless we can witness to our faith by words as well as by deeds.

Ideas and resources

Ideas

- Undertake a 'mission audit' by getting to know your own area. Study a map. Draw a sketch of the area, including the main roads, railways, etc. Draw lines across your sketch indicating the main boundaries around and within the area. Place symbols in each section, indicating the environment, e.g. house, tree, factory. Then prepare a local area survey and collect as much information as possible.
- Identify the suffering and struggling people in your area, and make the effort to meet at least one person or group. If you are working in a group then many more people may be contacted. Listen, learn, pray, act.
- Keep a file of newspaper cuttings of troubled spots around the world. Suggest a church notice-board for prayer, links and action. In a group make a list of suffering and struggling situations and people around the world. Listen, struggle to understand, pray, discuss possible action and act.
- Develop a link of friendship with an overseas Church, group, community or family.
- Identify a way in which you may learn from your link, e.g. if your link is in the less developed world you may learn from the way primary health care is being developed. Think about how such care could be encouraged in Britain.
- Identify a way in which you may help your link, e.g. educational ideas, offering magazines, books and other resources, etc.

Group Bible study

Read Luke 19.1–10.

Read the story of Jesus and Zacchaeus and allow time for quiet reflection.

- Act out the story in the group.
- Why did Zacchaeus change?
- What may we learn from this story about how to approach those who are oppressing others?

Resources

The Board of Mission
Church House
Westminster
London SW1P 3NZ

CMS and USPG
Partnership House
157 Waterloo Road
London SE1 8UU

Christians Aware
10 Springfield Road
Leicester LE2 3BD

Suggested reading

Charles Elliott, *Comfortable Compassion* (Hodder & Stoughton, 1987).
Naim Stifan Ateek, *Justice and Only Justice* (Orbis Books, 1989).
Living Faith in the City, a progress report by the Archbishop of Canterbury's Advisory Group on Urban Priority Areas (General Synod of the Church of England, 1990).
Leonardo Boff, *Good News to the Poor* (Burns and Oates, 1992).
Hans Küng, *Global Responsibility* (SCM, 1991).

Splattered hedgehogs

The heatwave continues and the latest casualties are the hedge-hogs. A note from an animal hospital warns us that hedgehogs are dehydrating and asks us to put out bowls of water for them. I look after two hedgehogs in my urban garden; the problem is making sure that they stay in the back garden and don't go around to the front.

Life is relatively secure in the back garden, and when the hedgehogs meet with any danger—a crow, a cat, a dog, a human being—they respond in the old instinctive way, they curl up into a ball, stick out their spines, and hope for the best. It's a defence that's served hedgehogs well throughout the centuries. It still works in the back garden; it's useless and dangerous out at the front drive. The drive fronts on to one of the busiest roads in London. It's a road where I not infrequently see a splattered and very dead hedgehog—for the world has changed and nobody has told the hedgehog. The old defence mechanisms are useless. The hedgehog senses danger, curls up into a ball, sticks out the spikes, and the next moment is hit by a juggernaut.

Very sad, and it's even sadder when the same thing happens to people, to nations, to Churches. We know how to curl up into a ball when danger threatens. We have plenty of sharp spikes which we can stick out which signal 'Keep off, keep off'. That defence has served us well for centuries, but the world has changed, and the juggernaut of history is crushing yesterday's instincts and solutions.

As a nation we're no longer a precious stone set in a silver sea which guards us like a moat from less fortunate folk, and carries our ships to far-flung empires. No, the moat is bridged, the walls are down, the tunnels are on the way. We're part of the main, and yesterday's nationalistic prickles are useless and dangerous.

As the Christian Church in this land we no longer have a monopoly of truth and goodness. Our next-door neighbours are Jews or Muslims, Sikhs or Hindus: we can, of course roll up into a ball, stick out our Christian prickles and throw biblical proof texts around, but in the new world which we have on our hands I suspect that God is more honoured in the open co-operation of people of faith than in prickly defensiveness.

Then in our working life, change is the order of the day. It used to be the case that we trained for a job and then lived out of that training for a lifetime, putting out professional prickles when anybody came near our territory. That's true no longer. Our college notes are dated the moment they're written.

The Bible doesn't say much about hedgehogs, but it says a good deal about change. God showed up as an unfailing source of support and strength to those prepared to go the way of God into the future and God showed up as an implacable enemy to those living out of past nostalgias. So let's feed and water the hedgehogs in this time of drought, but let's not copy them. The Lord of history wants to use us, not splatter us.

Section Three

Just Witness

The Bishop of Hyderabad in Pakistan gave one of the keynote addresses on the subject of mission at the 1988 Lambeth Conference. His lengthy and learned talk is part of the conference record, but the vivid story which he used to introduce his lecture is what remains in our minds.

The bishop explained that the Gospel was first brought to his people by an English doctor who established a small clinic on the main street of a certain village. Nobody went to him because they told themselves 'The English have failed to conquer us with their army, so now they are trying to poison us with this man's medicine'. After a few weeks a dog with a broken leg wandered into the clinic and the doctor, having time on his hands, cleaned the wound, bound it up with a splint and sent it on its way. The people watched the dog hobbling down the street and said to one another 'If this man is so good as to heal a worthless creature like a dog, then perhaps he will be good to us'. They began to use his clinic and eventually to hear his faith.

'Now', asked the bishop, 'who was the real missionary to my people? It was the dog! For the dog witnessed to where he had found healing.' He went on 'I call this "dogology" '.

This section will be full of such 'dogology' because we believe that 'just witness' is basically quite simple, it is witnessing to where we have found healing and leaving others to draw their own conclusions and make their own decisions, at the same time as recognizing that their experience may have been different and that we ourselves might learn from that. We are usually more comfortable when we are attempting to witness to our faith by our actions rather than by our words. But we need to question our hesitation about speaking about our faith. After all, in the earliest days of the Christian Church the bearer of the Gospel had nothing to offer the world but news of Jesus Christ and the challenge of accepting God's love and grace. The Church had no wealth, no schools to found, no clinics to open, no 'civilizing' mission to perform, just news about Jesus Christ, and it was this news which transformed the world.

We might ask whether Christians ever have the option of keeping the faith to themselves. It is integral to the Christian faith that it should be shared with others, for the sharing is part and parcel of our discipleship, as has been shown from the time of Jesus and the earliest Christians down through all the centuries of movement and mission. If Christian faith is not shared it will be distorted and the Church will become an inward-looking club. The Gospel is like the manna in the wilderness, it cannot be kept—if it is not used, it goes stale. We are frequently involved in interfaith dialogue and find that members of other world faiths are astonished when Christians are reluctant to talk about their faith and about why it inspires them. Perhaps this reluctance is a challenge to those of us who are Christian teachers to make more effort to offer useful, clear resources and teaching.

Witness is an indispensable element of Christianity. However, the way in which we witness to our faith must be consistent with the faith itself, and should reflect its graciousness. God loved and loves the world and not the little bit of it which became the Church. The cross is a sign of love and grace, it is not a club with which to beat non-believers, for we witness to a faith which is a promise, not a threat. When Vincent Donovan shared the Gospel with the Maasai people, one of them asked him whether God cared more for people in the Church than for the Maasai, and went on to say that if he did then he must simply be a tribal God. Vincent Donovan's experience with the Maasai led him to believe that the Maasai were a people loved by God and he shared his Christian faith with them because he knew that meeting Christ would enrich and enhance their lives. In turn he was himself enriched by encountering the Maasai approach to God. One of the values of inter-faith dialogue is that, when entered into honestly and openly, it offers the Christian an experience of learning with people of other faiths who are loved by God and who are, like all of us in the Church, good and bad. Dialogue offers enrichment and enlightenment for all who take part in it.

There is a story that when St Francis stood before Sultan Melek-el-Kamil of Egypt and preached the Gospel of Jesus Christ, the Sultan made a promise to him: 'Francis, if I ever meet another Christian as good as you, I will become a Christian myself.' He never did. There is another story of a Franciscan friar who was a chaplain with the Spanish forces when they captured Peru. He tried every way he knew to persuade Atahualpa, the Inca and a descendant of the Sun-god, to become a Christian, including argument and, in desperation, torture. Finally, his patience exhausted, the friar told the Inca that unless he agreed to be baptized he would be executed. The Inca said 'If I am baptized, when I die will I go to heaven?' 'Yes', promised the friar. 'And in heaven will I meet with other Christians like you?' 'Yes', said the friar. 'Then kill me now', said the Inca, 'for I never want to meet anyone as wicked as you.'

Terrible certainties are sometimes as unappealing as terrible doubts. This is why hard-sell evangelism does not always produce the hoped-for results, especially if it is divorced from humanity. The reason is not that those who proselytize enthusiastically are wicked, it is more that they send the signal to their hearers that they are not 'all there'. They have simplified the world and the Gospel to a caricature, and their fanaticism for it has become inhuman. They burn with enthusiasm in a way which is single-minded and often obsessive, so that they are unable to listen to others, even other Christians, and they cut themselves off from learning and growing. The hearer is bound to be secretly asking, like the Inca, do I want to be like this? And unless people are desperately poor, lonely or wounded, the answer is likely to be a polite 'No, thank you'.

Heresy is a word much out of favour today. But in past ages heretics were simply extremely keen Christians who had often seized upon what was true, but then by giving it exclusive importance, and by losing sight of balancing truths, they promoted it in a way which was distorting, misleading and even destructive. Christians who fling favourite texts around to support a narrow and dogmatic version of Christ's wide Gospel of grace and truth, are being heretical in this way, and need to be challenged.

There is an animal, the bamboo lemur, which has so specialized its eating habits that it can eat bamboo which has pith laced with cyanide because its stomach produces a chemical which is an antidote to the poison. The price it pays is that it can't eat anything else. If the bamboo goes, so does the lemur. There are Christians who have so narrowed their perspectives that their whole life is spent in or around the church or on their pet cause or charity. They might thrive on this diet but others are not usually tempted to follow their example, for they rightly see that such a narrow perspective would be poisonous for their own human and spiritual development.

The essence of the Gospel is that God loved us before we were lovable and demonstrated the unstoppable nature of that love in the life, death, triumph and glory of Jesus Christ. Christians, just as much as others, often find that good news too good to be true. They give the impression that God's love must be earned through good works or good faith, and they have prescriptions for both. God loves us into his kingdom, however, and invites us to join with him in loving others in. We must ever be witnessing to this love of God in the Christian community whose members so easily forget it. God only makes new Christians through Christians being made new. The Archbishop of York has said that the simplest definition of saving faith is 'the opening of ourselves to the ever present love of God in order to be changed by it'. We are called to become more like the God we worship, and through the grace of God to build a Christian community which lives in such a way that our neighbours find our faith attractive as well as challenging. If we haven't got the answer for Christians then it is unlikely that our gospel will be good news for anybody else.

When Billy Graham came to London in the late 1980s he was planning to have at least one of his gatherings in the East End of London. He had the sensitivity to realize that the East End has a strong culture all its own and so he arranged a meeting of local Church leaders to brief him. 'What shall I say to your people?', he asked. There was a wealth of advice and then the Roman Catholic Area Bishop, Victor Guazzelli, said 'Just tell them that God loves them. That's what they need to hear.' That surely is the heart of our own witness. Our task is not to save the world for Christ but to witness to the fact that God through Christ has loved us, and loves our neighbour. That's what we all need to hear.

God is already there

We do not take the message of God from the Church into a godless world, but we find God in the world as it is, good, bad and neutral. Through our life of prayer and witness we may open ourselves to God in our world and its people. We may compare notes, as it were, with our neighbours. We may be inspired by other people and by our world itself, its beauty and its needs, if we open ourselves to look, listen and learn. In this way both our faith and that of our neighbour may be strengthened and deepened. We may move away from the temptation of focusing upon ourselves, our faith, our prayers and our work, towards an outward-looking and creative partnership with God's people and God's world.

God has gone before us into his world, and is in the most seemingly hopeless places and situations as well as in the good and what seem to us to be 'promising places and people'. Our own Christian faith has been strengthened by the witness of suffering and struggling people around the world, who have managed to keep going and to have hope because they have known God to be with them in their needs and even in their losses and deaths.

We visited Sri Lanka when it was torn apart by the ethnic struggle and people were disappearing and then being found dead on the seashore or in rivers or ditches. We met mothers who had lost their children or husbands, and some mothers who had been so desperate that they had considered giving their children away. We met those who had lost their homes and were homeless in their own country, or were destitute in foreign lands, and we met people threatened with death for trying to bring peace. One of our friends, an Anglican priest, tried to bring the various conflicting groups together to talk and was so threatened that he had to leave his home with his wife and stay in a different house every night for over two years.

Another of our friends, who lives in Britain, received a letter from her mother who had to make a long and hazardous journey from Jaffna to Colombo, leaving relatives in danger in Jaffna. She wrote: 'The picture of Jesus and his cross is in my house, and he will oversee everything . . .' Many of the Sri Lankan people we met, of many faiths, are kept going, and are able to do brave things, because of their trust that God is with them. Their agonized lives and deaths are a powerful witness to God's enduring and abiding love.

The Bishop of Lebombo, Dinis Sengulane, wrote to a friend about the increased violence in Mozambique: 'The Lord gives us strength not to be as miserable as we would be if we were bearing the whole thing with our human unaided strength.'

When we visited Hong Kong we met people of many faiths who had grown used to a materially rich life-style, developed through trade and enterprise, but who are threatened with an unknown future after 1997, when Hong Kong will return to China. We were privileged to be guests of a Church in Hong Kong which is brave and determined to go on witnessing to the Christian faith into the future, and to be part of that future with all the people, even if sacrifices are called for, for God is in the change and movement as well as in what is still at the moment a safe place for them.

The people who know all about change and uncertainty are the Vietnamese people, the 'boat people', who camp precariously in Hong Kong detention centres, on islands and in boats, waiting for likely repatriation to what they see as a future of poverty and death. The camp we visited was for those who had been 'screened-out' and will be forced therefore to return to Vietnam, and yet the camp was bustling with life and hope. We should not have been surprised to see the makeshift chapels and shrines lovingly created in corners of the huts, witnessing to the fact that, for these refugees, God had not gone away but was still the centre of their life and hope. Faith, then, is not merely for the comfortable or for the safe or successful. We are able to experience God's presence in unhappy people, in their witness through their suffering and deaths, more than we sometimes experience it in successful and materially rich communities.

There is a poignant story of the group of Jews waiting for

death in a Nazi concentration camp. They were so appalled at the misery and injustice all around them that they put God on trial. The trial ended with God being found guilty. Then one of them, a rabbi, looked at his watch and said 'It is time for evening prayers', and off they went to pray to the God whom they had just condemned.

In another story of a similar Nazi camp a Jewish man was in despair as he saw the people being herded towards their deaths. 'Where is God in all this?', he wailed. 'There is God', replied his companion, pointing at the victims. This certainly would be the Christian understanding. We do not live in some Walt Disney world where the result of a life of faith is a happy ending, but nor do we worship a God who does not understand our doubt, pain and terror, for we believe that God has been to the darkest place on earth and was tortured to death on the cross. God's glorified body is also a scarred body. We would empathize therefore with the words scratched on the walls of an air raid shelter.

> I believe in light even when the sun does not shine. I believe in love even when love is not shown to me. I believe in God even when God seems to be absent.

It is this belief, in good times and bad, that we are called to share with others, helping them and ourselves to uncover the God who is already present in our lives and in the life of the world.

Gossiping the Gospel

The average Christian in Britain has a basic down-to-earth faith; sees authority in Scripture but is not too dogmatic about particular verses; worships undramatically Sunday by Sunday in the local church or chapel; and leads a useful and helpful life. Such a Christian is a little uncomfortable discussing the faith. It has been said that 'English Christians are like Canadian rivers in winter—frozen at the mouth'. A local churchman was by no means untypical when he said to his vicar at the start of the Decade of Evangelism 'I find all this talk about evangelism un-English—and anyway I thought that that was what you padres were paid to do'.

The good man has a point, of course. The word for 'evangelism' is only used three times in the New Testament. We are not all called to be evangelists. But we are all called to witness to our Christian belief, our own Christian story, and the strength and grace which are ours through our membership of the Christian Church. This witness is most authentic when it is a natural part of our lives. The words from St Matthew's gospel (28.19) are often quoted as giving the imperative for evangelism—'Go and make disciples of all nations'. But the actual words recorded by the evangelist have the meaning not so much of an order to 'Go!', but rather of advice on how to live, 'as you are going along in your journey through life take every opportunity to pass on the gospel'. Witnessing to our faith is an essential and natural part of holding that faith, it is a sharing with others which will enrich all who experience it.

Christians from other parts of the world are less inhibited than Western Christians in sharing their faith and they do it in vivid and creative ways, through music, drama and eloquent sermons. We have often been up till midnight in African homes because the families have wanted to sing and pray and share their stories. A great deal of the evangelism of young people in Africa is carried out through drama, and sometimes the Christian youth groups travel around from village to village acting out their commitment to their faith and to a Christian way of life.

When a group of young Kenyans was with us in England a few years ago they stayed with local Christians. Their hosts collected them from our house and took them to their homes. One of the young Kenyans went to stay with a devout university teacher and in the ten-minute drive to his home he made more impression upon him than a long life in the local church had done. He simply asked the good professor 'How did you become a Christian?' The professor had been a Christian all his life, but that question prompted him to start a reappraisal of his faith which was helpful and healthy.

We had to take a Tanzanian bishop to Heathrow airport. As he reached the head of the queue for weighing-in and booking a seat the young lady asked him 'Do you want a smoking or non-smoking seat?' 'What!' said the bishop. 'I'm a Christian; of course I don't want a smoking seat. I don't smoke or drink. Do you?' he asked the startled lady. 'Well', she stammered. 'Are you a Christian?' the bishop went on. By this time we were totally embarrassed, but the queue turned into a discussion group on the value of Christianity. What are we to make of all this? Do we English Christians shy away from witnessing to our faith directly because we are shy, or because we don't believe that it is the right thing to do? Our fellow Christians from around the globe have no such inhibitions and perhaps have a good deal to teach us in the Decade of Evangelism.

We need to be a little less shy about discussing our faith in public. Of course we will often get it wrong, because of our lack of knowledge or sensitivity, but God can use our inadequacies as well as our skills. Richard Adams, the founder of Traidcraft, tells of how he heard Christians talking about their faith when he was a fifteen-year-old boy. He thought to himself 'There's something in this, but they haven't got it quite right'. So started a journey of exploration of faith. We don't always need to have it quite right to start people on such an exploration. Indeed, sometimes we hardly know what words to use at all.

A young woman believed that she had been given a vocation to work as a missionary in Japan. Before she was accepted for training she visited the country and one day saw a girl working in the fields. She knew little Japanese but had one phrase which seemed to be appropriate. Shyly she said to the girl 'How beautifully you plant rice'. The girl smiled, the young woman smiled and went on her way. Three years later she was back as a missionary after her training. In church after a service a girl came up to her. 'Do you remember me? You spoke to me once. It was the first time anyone had appreciated anything I had done. I found out that you were connected with the church and now I have been baptized.'

Who knows where a gracious word to a neighbour will lead? The journey of faith, by its very nature, is more like a migration than a procession. People can start from where they are and move at their own pace. If they have any sense they will walk with the person who is seeking the truth of God, and avoid the person who believes that she has God's truth wrapped up and packaged. It is a basic mistake to regard the Christian journey as one in which some are more advanced than the others, who need to catch up. Jesus could be at his sharpest when correcting this misapprehension expressed by his disciples. He was more often a question to the answers of his followers than an answer to their questions. Our calling is to witness to the journey of faith, as we are, along its path, from where we are, and not to lay down detailed route maps for others to follow. People do not need preaching at, they need talking with and sharing with in the journey we are all, as people of faith, engaged in.

God and other faiths

The Decade of Evangelism has not been universally welcomed in Britain. Many are stressing the dangers of insensitive evangelism in a multi-faith society, the dangers of building additional barriers in an already divided society. Some Christians believe that there is a Gospel imperative for Christians to do their utmost to ensure that all people everywhere become Christian. Christians certainly believe that it will be the experience of all people, when they finally see God as God is, to discover that God is the God revealed by Jesus Christ. This is not the same, however, as insisting that all people must explicitly claim Jesus as their personal Lord and saviour in this life before they can approach God. Indeed the parable of the sheep and the goats in St Matthew's gospel (25.31f.) would warn us against any interpretation of salvation which relied totally upon claiming Jesus as Lord verbally. The test in that parable seems to be rather whether the hidden Christ in the prisoner, the hungry or the outcast is served—a very human test which would seem to be applicable to all humankind.

Christians may disagree therefore about whether in a multi-cultural society like Britain it is right or wrong to assertively evangelize practising members of other faiths; the fact is that such evangelism is rarely successful. Historically Christianity has hardly ever made significant inroads into cultures where there is a strong and living traditional faith. Even in the early days of the Church, Gentile converts to Christianity soon outnumbered those from Judaism. The number of converts from those with a living faith in Islam or Hinduism has again been modest. Those coming to Christianity historically have been those marginalized from strong faiths or in cultures where there is no longer a strong and adequate faith.

We see the same pattern today in England. People from all cultures are becoming Christians but they rarely come directly from having another living faith. Practising Hindus, Buddhists, Jews, Muslims or Sikhs are rarely converted. People who are converted are normally lapsed from their faiths, including Christianity, and they have often been lapsed for a whole generation. In Britain today, where a minority of people are regularly practising members of any faith, the lapsed are in the majority and it would seem to be sensible to focus the Church's evangelism in their direction.

Of course this does not mean that we should not have dialogue with those of other faiths for it is extremely fruitful to do so. By such dialogue we not only learn about what inspires the people of other faiths but we also deepen and broaden our own faith and build bridges of understanding with those with whom we should be working in building local community. It may be that out of dialogue some people might be moved to change their faith, but we should not as Christians seek to control them in such a change, for we believe that God loves them as he loves us, and we can safely leave their future to him. The World Council of Churches, gathering at San Antonio, wrestled with the question of dialogue with those of other faiths. The conference concluded 'We cannot point to any other way of salvation than Jesus Christ, at the same time we cannot set limits to the saving power of God'.

The Council of Churches for Britain and Ireland, through its Committee for Relations with People of Other Faiths, has produced a very helpful guide for the Churches on the four principles of inter-faith dialogue. The booklet, *In Good Faith*, aims to help Christians to dialogue with members of the other historic world faiths who are living in Britain. The four principles of dialogue are: dialogue begins when people meet each other; dialogue depends upon mutual understanding and mutual trust; dialogue makes it possible to share in service to the community; and dialogue becomes the medium of authentic witness.

Relationship with our neighbour according to these guidelines may begin with cultural courtesies but should go well beyond them. A Sri Lankan Christian tells of when he was living in central London. The house opposite seemed to be unoccupied but one evening an Indian lady knocked on his door, came in and gave him a little gift. She said that she and her husband had just taken up residence in the house. As is customary in the East, he dropped in at her home the next day and left a small gift for her son. In this simple act of sharing each had found a neighbour and a friend, and a Hindu had met a Christian in mutual respect.

The same man tells of how he had been invited by his Buddhist doctor to his daughter's engagement party. Buddhist monks recited from the scriptures, holy thread was distributed and other aspects of the ceremony were explained to the guests. Before the formal exchange of rings he was invited to say a few words and, apart from conveying his good wishes, he read the hymn on love from 1 Corinthians, chapter 13. Because a relationship of friendship had already been developed, it was possible for some of the profundity of the different faiths to be shared.

There are three main Christian theological viewpoints which are taken towards people of other faiths, which will obviously determine the approach made to them. The word 'exclusive' is used by those who believe that salvation is only through an explicit affirmation of Jesus Christ. The word 'inclusive' is used by those who believe that other people are saved through what God had done in Jesus Christ whether they affirm or realize it or not. The word 'pluralist' is used by those who believe that people are saved within their own tradition of faith whether Christian or not.

But is 'being saved' necessarily the most helpful concept in inter-faith dialogue? It is certainly a word well-used in some Christian circles, but less frequently in others. Vincent Donovan is only one of many Christians who, in Britain and around the world, having encountered people of another culture and faith in depth, could no longer say that those people were outside God's saving love. Holiness and discipleship are equally rich Christian ideals. Muslims are not so much interested in being 'saved' as in being obedient to the will of God, whilst the Christian concept of original sin is foreign to the Jewish tradition. We all, however, whatever our faith traditions, are fellow pilgrims in the world, facing the same deep questions about the meaning and purpose of life and death. In our search we can share our religious understandings and perceived truths with others. As Christians we must naturally share our treasure of the good news of Jesus Christ, but our religious vocabulary is not the only way of talking about God; in dialogue we must be ready to listen to the insights of others and, in doing so, expect to find that our own Christian faith is deepened and enriched by viewing it from a different perspective.

Our major witness surely needs to be in engagement with the spirit of an age which sees religious beliefs of any sort as being optional, private, problematical and even unnecessary. We must surely witness to our beliefs in a society where the Christian faith has sometimes been heard but is often rejected or ignored. Of course when people stop believing in traditional faiths, they do not usually then believe nothing, they tend to believe anything. We live in a world which is a market place of different beliefs and of none, where traditional faiths like Christianity, Islam and Hinduism jostle with new religions like Jehovah's Witnesses and the Unification Church, with off-shoots and sects which promise certainty and which deny people's reason, and with a variety of New Age philosophies which when unpacked from their modern wrapping seem to include many old ideas which previous generations have discovered led nowhere. The modern religious market place is a pick-and-mix of old and new ideas, and all too often they are swallowed in a pick-and-mix way—a bit from here, a bit from there—and the result can be shallow or sickening.

We should not be reluctant to enter into this market place of over-belief and under-belief. But neither should we be willing to see our rich, mature and vibrant faith trivialized by those who would believe too much or too little, or who would mix and stir the faiths so that their structure of holiness and demand is lost.

The Church's witness

The calling of the Christian Church must be to bring the good news of Jesus Christ into every stratum of society and through its influence to make all things new. There is always a twin danger in witnessing to our world. If we speak only from within the tradition and community of the Church, after a while we are speaking only to ourselves. If we speak only from contemporary secular society and ideas, then after a while we are merely a dull echo of passing trends. Even so the call to witness may be reasonably easy in Britain, where there is freedom of speech and action. It is a very different challenge however in many countries of the world, where there is no freedom at all and where Christian witness is sometimes against the law.

Some Christians in Britain are very clear about what the call to be Christian means in our own society. It means every lay Christian being a fine example of honesty and fair dealing in their business life, whilst seeking out fellow Christians at work and strengthening each other's faith in prayer, discussion and Bible reading. It means every Christian family being an example of fidelity and love. It means reclaiming our institutions and cities for Christ in 'Marches for Jesus'. The commitment of Christians who think like this cannot be denied, nor can the sincerity of their discipleship.

We would like to think that the witness of the Church to the institutions and structures of our society can be wider and deeper than this. Again we believe that God is there before us, that the Spirit of God is not exclusively the property of any Church, sect, or religion, but that all human institutions and peoples are both brushed by its wings and fail to capture it.

In an influential contribution to the debate on Mission at the 1988 Lambeth Conference, Bishop David Gitari from Kenya raised useful distinctions relating to the cultures of those to whom we go with the Gospel which were originally made by Bishop Stephen Neill. The distinctions are very useful touchstones for both local and global mission:

- There are some customs which the Gospel cannot tolerate and which therefore must be fought.
- There are some customs which can be tolerated for the time being.
- There are some customs which are fully acceptable to the Gospel and which therefore should be encouraged, strengthened and transformed.

In his own country Bishop Gitari included the examples of cattle stealing and twin-destruction as falling into the first group. Controversially, he suggested that polygamy and female circumcision fell into the second category and could therefore be lived with for the time being. (Not all the African bishops agreed with him in this.) He suggested that many customs associated with marriage, African hospitality and the community's relationship to the individual were in harmony with the Gospel and should be endorsed and transformed.

We find Bishop Gitari's categories helpful in relation to the Gospel and culture and also in relation to the Gospel connection with and relevance for every aspect of life. The categories offer a possibility of steering a path between those who would involve us in a continuous battle with our contemporary world, expecting us to join every movement of protest; and those decent people around the world who do not want to get involved in controversy and tell themselves 'They must know what they are doing and it isn't up to us to make a fuss'.

The first category—Fighting in the name of the Gospel

In the first category there are many examples of the Church and its members around the world resisting movements in society which they have seen as being against Gospel values.

The chapel to the Twentieth-Century Martyrs in Canterbury Cathedral is a memorial to some of the people who have given their lives in fighting and witnessing for justice against evil in many countries and situations. One of those remembered is Archbishop Oscar Romero who fought bravely in El Salvador against violence and death squads, and against an unjust social system of a few wealthy people squashing the poor and disease-ridden majority. Jon Sobrino has written of him 'He never ceased in his attack, he never tempered it, he never found prudent reasons for silence. Unlike others he never put the church's own security before the necessity of attacking repression.' Two weeks before he died, in March 1980, Oscar Romero said in an interview 'A bishop may die, but the church of God, which is the people, will never die'. Many members of the Church in El Salvador have continued to be brave and to die in striving for Gospel values, most recently, in November 1989, the six Jesuits from the University of Central America with their housekeeper and her fifteen-year-old daughter. The year before their deaths the Jesuits had helped to organize a national debate on the desperate need of the country for peace with justice. The Roman Catholic Church, which produced Archbishop Romero, the Jesuits and many other people who have fought obvious evils in El Salvador, must surely believe that their deaths have contributed enormously to the 1992 peace accord.

The Roman Catholic Church fights a consistent battle against anything in Western culture which it sees as cheapening human life. That Church in particular has a great antipathy to abortion and euthanasia, and also has great anxieties about genetic engineering. Many other Christians share this view, while many others, Roman Catholics amongst them, feel that none of these issues has an absolute all-or-nothing ethical tone. Bishop Gitari's own illustrations make it very clear that Christians will not always agree about which issues fit into which categories. It is good that the Church should struggle to find a way forward in acting as a conscience to the world and in so doing ensuring that society will not go down an inhuman road without awareness.

The Episcopal Church in America took a firm stance against its government's determination to go to war in the Gulf. The Church people felt that this decision was being taken long before all other avenues had been explored and they strove, unsuccessfully, to hold the Gospel imperative of peace-making before their nation.

In a world of large power-blocs and multi-national corporations, sometimes our witness to Gospel values has to be made in a global arena. We personally have recently been drawn into the debate at the General Synod and beyond concerning the marketing practice of some large baby-milk manufacturers in donating free supplies of their products to maternity units in developing countries. At first sight this might seem to be a generous act and it undoubtedly has a place at times and in places of great emergency. As a standard marketing practice, however, with or without the agreement of the national governments, it is fraught with danger.

From our time of living in Africa we were aware of some of the facts of bottle feeding which are well known to nutritional specialists. We knew that a bottle-fed child in the less developed world is twenty-five times more likely to die than a breast-fed child. There are several reasons. The lack of clean water and fuel for fires makes it very difficult for a mother to provide the sterile conditions for mixing the baby milk powder and giving it to her child in a clean bottle. The chance of the child developing enteritis, therefore, is very great indeed. Then there is the expense of the baby-milk powder. The mother only discovers this after her baby has become used to the 'free' milk in the hospital and her own milk has consequently dried up from lack of use. Once at home, however, with the milk powder needing to be paid for, the mother often overdilutes the product so that it will go further. The child then runs into the danger of becoming malnourished and consequently of having little resistance to disease.

The needs of the vulnerable have a high place in the Gospel message and Jesus Christ often referred to the innocence and defencelessness of children. It is not surprising then that, like many other Christian groups around the world, the General Synod agreed that this was an issue which must be tackled head-on. Indeed, to emphasize the depth of its concern the Synod passed a resolution that one of the most popular products of one of the major world manufacturers should be boycotted.

The second category—Tolerating for the sake of the Gospel

According to Bishop Gitari's second category there are many situations which Christians would ideally wish to change but which can be tolerated for the time being. He has told the story of the nineteenth-century chief of a West African tribe who heard the Gospel from missionaries and asked for baptism. However, the chief was told that if he wished to be baptized he could only have one wife, and all the others must go. Thus, to the African chief, the good news became bad news, so instead of sending the wives away he sent the missionaries away and became a Muslim. The canon on marriage of the Church of the Province of Kenya now tolerates those who were polygamists before they became Christians, so that they may be baptized with their believing wives and children. This does not mean that the Church encourages or approves of polygamy, but that it recognizes that the expelling of already existing wives and children is a worse evil than polygamy.

An example of the British Churches of all denominations

working with the nation in a situation which had to be tolerated was both during and after the Falklands War. Many Church people in Britain had shared the general view that the war had been fought for a just cause but were also distressed by the many casualties which modern warfare brings. The Church leaders who planned the service in St Paul's Cathedral after the war were determined that the dominant spirit should be one of reconciliation and graciousness to a former enemy. And so it proved. There were those who might have preferred to see a more triumphal approach to the service, but the Church on this occasion acted as the conscience of the nation and so enabled the nation to move forward into a future which must always include the reconciliation of previous foes.

Occasionally, what has been seen as an ethically neutral situation changes. The Kenyan Anglican Church since independence has been very supportive in working with others, including the government, in the task of nation building and development. They might have had hesitations about the development of the one-party state but this has not until recently become a major point of public friction. Some Church leaders in recent years, however, perceived an increasingly undemocratic regime developing. One of them, Bishop Alexander Muge, expressed his belief that these developments were hostile to the Gospel values of human dignity and freedom. He did so with such vigour that many people believed that he was putting his life in danger. He was indeed shortly afterwards killed in a car crash. Many recent developments in Kenya have helped the movement to a more democratic form of government. The brave contribution of Christians like Alexander Muge has strengthened the country in its rethinking.

The third category—Encouraging in the service of the Gospel

Bishop Gitari said in his third category that the Church should discern those aspects of life which are fully acceptable to the Gospel and which should be endorsed and transformed. Shortly before independence in Zambia, the British colonial government selected those African leaders and civil servants who they thought would be likely to hold senior office in the newly independent nation. They sent them to embassies all over the world, giving them an accelerated programme of training to prepare them for their new responsibilities. The government did not think about the equally dramatic changes which would be coming the way of the wives and families of these ministers and civil servants.

The Mothers' Union did think of this. They knew that it is very often the woman who holds and develops the family's traditions and culture and what goes for a family goes for a nation. In addition they realized that many of these women would be involved in offical duties both at home and in embassies around the globe and that they needed to be prepared for this. The MU set up a training programme at an ecumenical institute in Zambia, as demanding as what was offered to the men in Washington or London. This imaginative initiative on the part of a Church organization made a great contribution to the transitional process of nation building just when it was needed. It was a great act of Christian witness which did not go unnoticed.

In Britain the Church was very much involved in the recent debates concerning educational reform. The Church of England and the Roman Catholic Church have many hundreds of Church schools within the state system of education and so they have a wealth of 'hands-on' experience. The Church was well placed, therefore, from this traditional position of educational partnership, not only

to make general statements in principle about the pro-
posed reforms, but to argue in detail, point by point, concerning the legislation. This was not confined to matters of
religious education, but of course the Church had particular
wisdom and experience to contribute over this. It was able
to stand with those of all religious faiths who had become
disturbed by the way in which religious education had been
diluted to such an extent that it had almost disappeared in
many state schools. The Church did not agree with those
Christians who believed that in a 'Christian' country like
Britain Christianity alone should be taught in our schools.
Religion can be a source of strength or division in a society.
Getting the balance between educating our children to
respect the traditions of all the faiths which make up our
society and at the same time understanding in some detail
the religion, Christianity, which has most helped to mould
it, is not easy, but that is what the Church sought for, and
to some extent achieved, in the new Act. In any event, the
process was a good example of the Church and society working in partnership in order to achieve basically agreed
ends.

The Gitari categories are not always hard and fast, however. The great theologian Karl Barth once wrote a book
entitled *I Changed My Mind*. So the Church and Christian
groups occasionally, on reflecting more deeply on their
Christian heritage and teaching, change their minds about
what in society is harmful, neutral, or helpful to Gospel
values.

A supreme example of this change of mind has been that
of the white Dutch Reformed Church in South Africa in its
attitude to apartheid. For many years this Christian group
provided a convoluted spiritual and intellectual support to
the apartheid system. The separate African, Coloured,
Indian and white Dutch Reformed Churches had developed
in the mid-nineteenth century from fear of offending
people if the Churches were united. With such a history the

Dutch Reformed Church had no trouble in supporting apartheid in 1948. The attitudes of this Church over more than a century are in fact a great warning of the dangers for any church or group of living, thinking, acting and praying in isolation from those around and from the wider world. Most other denominations in South Africa have always seen apartheid as being evil and many Christian men and women of all races have given their lives in fighting it. The protests of the South African Council of Churches have been, especially in the recent years of non-violent direct action, sacrificial and very public.

The Dutch Reformed Church bravely changed its mind and withdrew its ethical undergirding for an unbiblical ideology for many reasons, including the pressure of the Indian, African and Coloured Dutch Reformed Churches and the example of most other South African Christians. The November 1990 conference at Rustenburg saw all the main South African Church groupings joined together in denouncing apartheid and in committing themselves to a multi-racial future for South Africa.

We hope the future South Africa may grow and develop as a truly African community which is also multi-racial, where the individual does not exist without the community, where life is not compartmentalized, where there is no division between religious, social, cultural and economic life; but where each area affects the others, and where the witness of Christians to the values of the kingdom of God, of love, joy and peace, permeates them all.

The style which we have been advocating in this section might well be called the 'On the Road to Gaza' principle of witness, after the story in the Acts of the Apostles (8.26–40), where Philip shared the Gospel with the Ethiopian eunuch as they travelled along. It is a style which does not so much preach at people as share their story and our own Christian story, and then if they wish introduce them into the community called Church, which is ever deepening our knowledge of God and pointing us to the service of God's world. But whether or not people choose to join our community of faith, we must work with them in building the 'community of communities' which we need if the world is to be passed on to our children and grandchildren.

Ideas and resources

Ideas

- Write your own Christian story. One way of doing this is to prepare a chart, perhaps including photographs.
- Write prayers, poems or stories to communicate your faith or an aspect of it.
- Identify three people who have witnessed to you about their Christian faith. Reflect, either alone or in a group, upon what you have received from the three.
- Make a list of the responses of your church to the Decade of Evangelism. In a group discuss ways in which these responses will be good news to those they are initiated for.
- Develop opportunities for sharing your faith with those of other faiths at the same time as you listen to them telling you about their faith.
- Consider visiting the chapel of Twentieth-Century Martyrs in Canterbury Cathedral.

Group Bible study

Read Acts 8.26–40.

- What was Philip doing when he began to speak about his faith?
- Why was the Ethiopian eunuch ready for Philip's interpretation and witness?
- What was 'good news' for the eunuch in Philip's conversation?
- What happened then?
- Speculate about the subsequent career of the eunuch.
- What does the group learn from the story about its own life and witness?

Resources

The Decade of Evangelism Steering Group
Board for Mission
Church House
Westminster
London SW1P 3NZ

Suggested reading

John D. Davies, *The Faith Abroad* (Basil Blackwell, Oxford, 1983).

Choan-Seng Song, *The Compassionate God* (SCM Press, 1982).

Vincent Donovan, *Christianity Rediscovered: An Epistle from the Maasai* (SCM Press, 1982).

Paul Knitter, *No Other Name?* (SCM Press, 1985).

Board of Mission, *Good News in Our Times* (Church House Publishing, 1991).

In Good Faith: The Four Principles of Interfaith Dialogue (The Committee for Relations with People of Other Faiths, Council of Churches for Britain and Ireland, 35–41 Lower Marsh, London SE1 7RL; 1991).

The Committee for Relations with People of Other Faiths, *Christian Identity, Witness and Interfaith Dialogue* (CCBI, 1991).

Jonathan Sacks, *The Persistence of Faith* (Weidenfeld and Nicolson, 1991).

Frogs

I once was involved in a scientific research project. We were trying to help those with hearing and sight difficulties by designing equipment to pick up minute electrical signals from the brain; and as a preparation for our work I spent hours in the library reading the latest reports.

Now all this was a few years ago; bishops, after all, have enough trouble worrying about their own headaches without finding time to investigate those of others, but I remember one of the bits of useless information which I learned about the brain of a frog. Did you know that out of our glorious Technicolour world, frogs only see three things: circles, blobs, and shadows? Everything else is eliminated by the frog brain as being of no interest, because it is of no use.

Why does the frog choose to just see circles, blobs, and shadows? Because circles mean security; blobs mean food; and shadows mean danger. The frog has to be able to recognize circles in order to hop from one safe leaf to the next. The frog has to be able to recognize blobs, because a blob might well mean the next free lunch, a juicy fly. And a frog must be sensitive to shadows, because this might mean the enemy—a swooping bird. So to the frog, the world is just made up of circles, blobs, and shadows; very sensible, but very sad.

There are times when people can seem to be a little frog-like, sensible but blinkered. Hopping from one circle to another: home, train, colleagues, friends, home, and never making the effort to engage with the stranger. Then, being alert for succulent blobs, the main chance, the juicy killing, the obviously useful, but missing the food which might nourish the heart and soul. And of course, always living in fear of the shadow: the swooping critic, the cutting remark which reopens old wounds. All very sensible, but rather sad—not really the life in abundance which God promises us.

How different from the people I was with last week. They were on a ten-day walking pilgrimage to Canterbury Cathedral. They came from churches dedicated to St Dunstan from all over the world and they were marking the thousandth anniversary of St Dunstan's death. In the vanguard, striding out, were a group of blind men from St Dunstan's Homes. And never was a group more full of life, energy and hope; walking fearlessly across field and hillside, sharing food and spare socks; blinded by war they might have been, but they made the world glow with colour.

I don't know what St Dunstan would have made of them, but they made me resolve to try to treat my life rather more like a pilgrimage of hope and promise, and rather less like a pond for the nurture of overweight frogs.

Section Four

Just Spirituality

There are basically three ways of being religious. First, religion can be used as a means to another end. For example, it can be the driving force behind social revolution or it can be the heart and soul of the cultural identity of a people, particularly if they are a minority group in a larger society. It can be a means to artistic expression—indeed in past centuries it was one of the major patrons of the arts. It can be a means to inner psychological experience—safer and cheaper than becoming involved in the drug culture.

Second, religion can be an end in itself. It can bring freedom from loneliness, doubt and fear, or from self-destructive behaviour. Some tightly controlled religious groups are very successful in changing the behaviour of their members. But members of such religious groups often discover that this freedom has been obtained at the cost of bondage to the group and its system of beliefs. It is not necessary, however, to be a member of such a religious group for religion to become an end in itself; every parish church and every clergy chapter contains people for whom this is so—who eat, drink, sleep, think and talk religion.

Yet there is a third way of being religious which is seeing religion as a quest, a journey of discovery to God and with God, turning God-talk into God-walk. It is this way of religion which we would want to call spirituality, a religion which is God-centred and this-worldly. On this journey of discovery we expect God to both guide us and goad us. We expect that there will be times of difficulty and darkness when we will long for the certainty which a tight religious faith which is an end in itself would promise us. But faith is not certainty. Faith is a trustful walk with God into the future, which is his secret.

The poetic biblical story of Adam and Eve in the Garden of Eden is often interpreted in terms of humankind's rebellion against God. Ambivalence over sex and sexual roles is mixed up with the detailed components of the story about the apple and the fig leaves. In fact the story tells us that the temptation was to eat the apple and be ' . . . like God and know what is good and what is bad'. In other words the temptation was to have certainty. Grasping after certainty is still our temptation and we still pay a high price for our search for it. What we are offered, freely and graciously by God, is faith, and if we are wise we will make do with that, and leave certainty to God.

Christianity was born at a time and in a place where three worlds were meeting—the East, the West and the world of Judaea. Through this meeting, and in a quite unconscious way, a rich and satisfying faith emerged which is a fulfilment of the hopes and expectations of all these worlds: of the mystical personal experiences of the East; of the idealistic rigour of the Greeks; and of the down-to-earth biblical pragmatism of the Jewish people. Out of these traditions emerged a Christianity which was God-centred and this-worldly, a religion which is ever making everyday life transparent to the Spirit of God, and at the same time rooting religious experience firmly back into the claims and duties of everyday life. 'Tell us what Christianity is, Bishop, you've got seven seconds', said the TV interviewer at the end of a programme. Is there an answer? 'Love God, love your neighbour through the grace of Jesus Christ.' It is a deceptively simple answer, and yet it is rich enough to take the journey of a lifetime with God to explore.

The archetypal religious journey is the legendary forty-year-long journey of Moses and the people of Israel across the desert. The journey started for Moses with a vision of the promised land and ended with his bird's-eye glimpse of it from the top of Mount Nebo. This is the authentic beginning and ending for a spirituality which is a religious quest for God. Olive Schreiner described the same quest by telling the story of a hunter who, whilst hunting for wildfowl, reached a lake where a huge shadow fell over him and he saw a cloudy reflection in the water. From that moment he was overcome by the desire to hold the vast white bird whose reflection he had glimpsed. His friends thought that he was mad. At last he set off in search of the bird, which was truth; leaving his security and entering a time of loneliness and danger as he travelled across unknown lands and up huge mountains, until the years passed and he was old and lay dying on the mountainside. A white feather fluttered down and he died holding it.

Having and following a vision of the promised land is not the same as building castles in the air. Many people, of course, make a good living out of spinning tales of dream castles and renting them out to those who from their loneliness or despair are yearning to escape to a better life. Other people are rigidly down to earth and are very quick to throw rocks at any dream castles in the air. Neither approach is ideal.

In the film *Man of La Mancha*, the poet Cervantes has been arrested and is placed in a deep dungeon where he waits to be interviewed by the Inquisition. While he waits he writes poetry, which annoys the ordinary criminals who are his fellow inmates. 'You must be mad, dreaming dreams, instead of coming to terms with things as they really are', one of them says to him. Cervantes replies 'When I see the suffering all around, who knows where madness lies? It might be mad to accept the suffering without protest, and it might be maddest of all to see things as they really are rather than as they might be.'

To see things as they really are, also to have a vision of how they might be, and to be prepared to play a part in building a world renewed by God, for God, is the start of the religious journey which is true spirituality. Lionel Blue in a TV programme about Wilberforce insisted that evil, sin and hell really exist, because we inflict all of them on one another. But he also claimed that heaven is real, provided we pay for it with our life as Wilberforce did. 'That's the great difference between real religion and pop religion', he went on. 'Pop religion is just a feeling and anybody can have a religious feeling. You can have it on the cheap anytime you want. But it only becomes real religion when you devote your life to opening an instrument of torture, and release a fellow human being into the light.'

Moses had a vision of a promised land of freedom for his people. He devoted his life to releasing them from their slavery in Egypt and to getting them to that promised land. It was not an easy journey of faith and there were many times when the temptation to turn back was great, but he kept going on, and on. He was inspired and encouraged by springs in the desert; walks with God; the community of grace; and glimpses of the promised land. Moses was kept going by what we suggest are ingredients of contemporary spirituality, in the religious journey which is neither an end in itself nor a means to other ends, but which is a quest, a quest towards a world transformed.

Springs in the desert

The people of Israel discovered on their journey that no matter how barren the desert, or featureless the landscape, day by day they were fed with manna from heaven, and day by day they were able to drink new life from springs in the desert. We all need our springs in the desert, our spiritual refreshment to give us the life, energy, direction and new direction for our journey of faith.

The spring in the desert is an absolute prerequisite for life to continue there at all. Some springs are fairly obvious, but some are more hidden, and it is as we go on and on in our journey that we are likely to be sensitive to them, to be kept alive by them and thus to be given the strength and the vision to see the special beauty in what was previously dull and ordinary.

The obvious place where Christians look for spiritual refreshment is in the biblical word. In the film *Lawrence of Arabia* Lawrence and his Arab companions have travelled between two wells across a particularly fearsome piece of desert only to discover that one of their number is no longer with them. Lawrence's companions shrug their shoulders, 'It is written', they say. 'It is not written', snaps Lawrence and turns back into the desert to seek the one who is lost. He returns many hours later, having found the man still alive. The others gasp in amazement and from then on Lawrence is known to them as 'The one for whom it is not written'.

Christians are people of faith for whom 'the Word' both written and not written provides daily springs in the desert. We may regard Bible study as a conversation with God, and Bible reading as God preaching to us, and like any sermon sometimes it will catch fire in our hearts and sometimes it won't. We do not limit God's word, there in the beginning and until the end of all things, to the words of the Bible of course. The words of God in the Bible are most likely to become a source of new life when they are translated and transformed by the Word of God incarnate in Jesus the Christ. And God is quite capable of speaking in many words and in many ways, if we are sensitive enough to hear his voice and open enough to listen and grow.

Like tens of thousands of people around the world, when we lived in Africa we used to switch on the radio each evening to hear the eight o'clock news from the World

Service of the BBC, a service highly regarded for its objec-
tivity. Tuning in to the World Service was no easy matter.
The signal was weak and was often swamped by the caco-
phony of music and voices from other stronger stations.
After a while, however, we learnt to pick up the station from
the merest hint of a voice. The style was quite distinctive,
even when it was no more than a distorted whisper. Tuning
in became a habit.

So it can be when we seek to hear the word of God amidst
the clamour and noise of our life and times. We can help
ourselves by creating a routine of ways and means and
whens. Karl Barth once wrote 'Any person who wants to live
responsibly must read two things, the Bible and the daily
newspaper, and never one without the other'. It is excellent
advice to put the daily Bible reading alongside the reading
of the newspaper, to throw in the diary for good measure,
and then to listen to God. Those who can find a regular
time and quiet place at home for this will soon come to find
great inspiration from it. Any place will do however, even
stopping the car in a lay-by on the way to work and 'tuning
in to God' may reveal a strong spring in the desert.

There was a time when daily 'tuning in to God' was the
basic spirituality of the people of England, and the same is
still true of most people of all faiths around the world today.
The vast majority of the people of India for instance still see
their religion as the most important aspect of their lives,
as what makes them what they are. In England the Book of
Common Prayer enabled a spirituality which could bring
about a slow growth from within Christianity over the years.
There were to be no first- and second-class Christians. There
was to be no great distinction between those who were 'religious' and those who were involved in ordinary life. The
spirituality was the same for all, a daily round of morning
and evening prayer based around biblical readings, psalms
and canticles; a weekly rhythm of praise, preaching and
sacrament; and the whole round of prayer and praise sup-

ported by a sensible, sensitive and consistent pastoral ministry. At its best this tradition provided a spirituality of
thoughtful holiness.

Twentieth-century folk in the West have largely turned
away from traditional and regular Christian spirituality.
Perhaps it is too demanding in an increasingly urban and
mobile society. But this does not mean that people have
embraced atheism, which may also be too hard for our soft-
centred society. In Britain five million people still go to
church regularly, whilst over fifteen million people tune in
to religious hymn-singing on television. Most of our fellow
citizens believe in God even if they do not believe in the
Church.

Our task as Christians is to uncover the springs in the
desert for our society as well as for ourselves; to uncover
the sacred values which still exist even if they are sometimes buried beneath materialistic or sentimental junk,
and to make the connections between the sacred and the
secular which will open the door to a holistic approach to
life.

When people make their occasional visits to church,
bringing their births or marriages or deaths, they are
acknowledging that if anything is sacred then 'this is', and
they are bringing the sacred moment to be validated and
handled. Of course on such an occasional basis they will not
get everything from our services and sacraments which we
may wish them to have, but they are usually open to catch
something of God's love and grace, and this should not be
denied them.

There is a story of a great nineteenth-century preacher
who heard of a very poor woman in his area, who was being
evicted from her cottage because she could not pay the rent.
After the Sunday evening service he took the collection,
walked to her cottage and knocked on the door. He knew
that the woman was inside the cottage but she would not
answer the door because she was afraid. She thought he was

the rent-collector coming with demands, or the bailiff coming with threats to evict her. He had to go away without giving her the gift he had brought for her.

Our task as Christians is to enable as many people as possible to open the door to the gifts of God and his kingdom. We cannot do this by behaving as if we were rent-collectors with our demands or bailiffs with our threats. In one of his novels William Golding describes a Religious Education lesson in which the teacher tries to instil the good news into one of her recalcitrant pupils by slapping him three times around the head at the same time as shouting 'God is Love'. A similar impact is often made on people who come to our churches for the first time for weddings, funerals, baptisms, or simply to escape from the rain. We once attended a service held in support of human rights around the world during which a tramp was evicted. We have very often attended wedding services when the only informal greeting of the priest to the congregation has been 'Do not throw confetti in the churchyard'. Many parents try to come to a church to have their baby baptized only to have what seem to them almost impossible demands placed upon them. The polar opposite attitude of complete indifference to people is not very likely to open them to God either. One couple who went along to their local parish church to request baptism for their baby were simply told 'Don't sit too near the back of the church'.

We in the Church often seem to be a long way away from communicating our great vision of the kingdom of God, perhaps because we are ourselves a long way away from the harmony and love we see portrayed in the Trinity. We ourselves are like the old woman who locked the door on the gift. The challenge towards mission is largely a challenge to openness, to listening, to God and to the God in others, to allowing the Spirit of God to work in us, not usually as we have planned and not necessarily as we would like. If we are open to God we are open to being surprised by his springs in the desert, we are open to moments of grace and moments of new possibility.

Walks with God

Moses was kept going in the journey through the wilderness to the promised land by his occasional walks with God. In such walks the faith is deepened, the vision clarified, or even given new direction. There are places in the gospels where Jesus is inspired by God to admit new ways of looking at people and at the world. The story of Jesus' encounter with the Syro-Phoenician woman begins with him refusing to help her because he does not see himself having a mission to the gentiles. The story ends with Jesus changing his attitude and helping the woman, surprised perhaps by her understanding and faith in him. Jesus' openness to a new idea enabled him to change direction, and in the long run to point the early Church on a journey outwards from its origins.

Sometimes this 'walk with God', is literally a walk—a pilgrimage, alone or with others in fellowship, thought, and dialogue. In fact going on pilgrimage is integral to many world faiths, including our own. The Sanskrit word *vandana* connects pilgrimage with worship. Adam's Peak in Sri Lanka is a place of pilgrimage worship for Buddhists, Hindus, Muslims and Christians. People of all the faiths join the pilgrimages to Adam's Peak, walking through the wet and jungly lower slopes and then up the steep and rocky paths. They sleep overnight in caves and greet the rising of the sun before moving off to the summit of the peak. We have walked along the Pilgrims' Way between Glastonbury and Canterbury, two of the Christian holy places of England. We have worshipped in beautiful and famous buildings, in tiny village churches, in people's gardens and in open fields; and we have understood a little of what some of our African friends have often said. 'Religion is not a department of life. Religion is life itself.'

Any real pilgrimage involves physical stretching and risk as well as spiritual stretching and challenge. In Murang'a Cathedral in Kenya there are murals on the gospel stories seen through Kikuyu culture. One of the murals depicts the birth of Jesus in the setting of the Kenyan emergency in the early 1950s. Down in one corner are three figures bearing essential gifts for the new baby, and they are three wise women, for men would never attend a birth in Kikuyu culture. The women are seen making their journey through dangerous territory, when villages were fenced off and placed under armed guard, and when those outside risked attack and death. The wise women went to the baby in spite of the risks, as in Kenya and all over the less-developed world today people make journeys and take risks to bring new life.

In northern Britain the early Celtic Christians walked for very long distances to share their faith. Many of them went through dangerous areas of heavily wooded countryside which was infested with wolves and other wild beasts. The earliest Christians went on risky pilgrimages to the Holy Land, walking into the river Jordan as Jesus had done, and visiting many of the places connected with Jesus' life and death. Modern visits to the Holy Land sometimes lack the element of risk. Many parish groups cancelled their visits during the Gulf War and sadly lost the opportunity to be real pilgrims, vulnerable and open to God. The people who live in the Holy Land also felt neglected and forgotten at a time when they needed friendship and support from outside the Middle East. One of our walks between Glastonbury and Canterbury was in honour of St Dunstan's Millennium in 1988. It was a long walk, and for those who were walking for the first time, like Canon Dunstan Bukenya from Uganda, it was both risky and painful. After the pilgrimage was over Dunstan wrote of 'the pain inside my boots', and went on '. . . I could not fit inside my sleeping bag and I never slept at all'. One of St Dunstan's own prayers was a help to us all.

> On the road to Emmaus, they thought Thou wast dead,
> Yet they saw thee and knew Thee in breaking of bread;
> Though day was far spent, in Thy face there was light;
> Look down on us gently, who journey by night.

Pilgrimages are normally embarked upon in community, so that the pilgrims learn from and help each other as trust develops. A mixed group of pilgrims provides the best opportunity for learning and growing. We have walked on multi-faith, ecumenical and international pilgrimages. The St Dunstan's pilgrimage included a large group from America, a group from Canada, Dunstan Bukenya from Uganda, and British people of all ages. A group of men blinded on active service also came from the St Dunstan's society. They were first-class walkers, and they also had very special experiences to share. The community, described by one of its members as 'weak and strong, proud and humble, sociable and solitary', developed as it journeyed on, and it was also constantly opened outwards and enriched by daily comers and goers, and by the communities we visited along the way. On a different occasion we climbed Mount Kenya with a European and Kenyan group, and had wonderful opportunities to help each other and to learn. We are told that Kenyan men will not cook, and will always therefore remember the Kenyan man who got up in the middle of the night to cook breakfast for everyone before we all set off to climb the mountain peak.

Pilgrims learn from each other and they also share with and learn from the people they meet along the way. The St Dunstan's pilgrimage took us into many and varied communities and families and gave us the opportunity to discuss issues facing the world with people of all ages and backgrounds. We met both old people and children at one hospice, and one of the children wrote afterwards 'I thought that the blind people were very brave walking such a long way. The guide dogs were nice as well.' Pilgrims may sometimes provide the moment of truth for those they meet, simply by being there as a group. We remember one multifaith walk through London, which included people of many of the world faiths and which took us to the places of worship of the people. When we arrived at one church the priest was very cold and did not wish to pray with us, but stood at the back of the church. As the prayers went on, however, he gradually edged his way down one of the aisles until he was at the front, welcoming everyone, sharing in the refreshments and establishing friendships. One of our pilgrimages included British and South African people and took us through many communities as we walked to London on the anniversary of the Sharpeville shootings in South Africa, in support of democracy and justice there. At the end of one parish meeting a woman stood up and announced that her son and his family were living in South Africa. She said that she had been wrong to accept the situation and that she would write at once and tell them to come home.

Going on pilgrimage offers the pilgrim opportunities for meeting herself as well as other pilgrims and people along the way. And through and with all the journeys and all the meetings is the meeting with God. For Moses the mountain was often the place of meeting. Sometimes this was at God's invitation, sometimes Moses took the initiative. We like the story of when Moses was up the mountain grumbling to God about the wretched people God had given him to lead. The dialogue perhaps went a little like this. God said 'I know, Moses, they are a dreadful people, and it's worse than you think because whilst you are up here grumbling to me, they are down there making a golden calf to worship. I tell you what we'll do. We'll wipe them out and start again with better material.' This of course brought Moses to his senses:

'Nobody wipes my people out. It's my job to get them to the promised land, and to the promised land they'll go.'

The conversation then clarified Moses' vision. And we need to give space in our own lives for such walks with God, walks in which God can guide us and goad us. The retreat movement is popular. It is not essential however to get away to a holy place or to go on pilgrimage to walk with God. A reflective walk around the park, a visit to a cathedral, an afternoon at home set aside for thought and prayer, may all provide meetings on the mountain top for us.

Sometimes out of such meetings we may, like Moses, come away carrying new codes of behaviour, sometimes we can expect to have had our faith strengthened or challenged as we are faced with new moments of truth. This will not always be comfortable. Charles Elliott once described how he had been conducting the morning and evening worship for a national conference. He provided a variety of ways of worshipping on the basis that God calls some people with a shout, some with a song, and some with a whisper. He could see that not everyone was appreciating the variety he offered. One of the participants came to him late in the evening and asked to speak to him. He made an appointment to see her after breakfast and morning worship the next day. She duly came to his room. 'Now', she said, 'I haven't been able to get on with your worship. At least, not until this morning. This morning you said "Let us sit in silence and listen to what God is saying to us". I did, and God said to me "For Pete's sake grow up!" God has never spoken to me like that before, what do you think it means?'

In our walks with God, God will not infrequently challenge us to grow up, because God, while having an accurate understanding of what we are, also has a clear vision of what we might be, and through his grace provides us with the means of becoming it. When we grasp this, it is difficult for us not to be dissatisfied with what we are. Wilberforce in one of his encounters with God, when the faith caught fire in a more vibrant way in his life, wrote 'If this is true then it is madness to live a trivial life'. The Bishop of Durham tells us that 'God is a spirituality upholding all things, enfolding all things, penetrating to the heart of all things, but . . . Jesus comes as disturbance and will return as disturbance. We get him wrong and think of him as a comfort, but he is only a comfort when he is first accepted as a disturbance.'

Community of grace

The third element which kept Moses going on his journey into God's future across the desert towards the promised vision was the people God had given him to travel with— the community of grace, his fellow pilgrims. Look around the average church congregation and you see an average cross-section of local folk, perhaps with a larger proportion of the elderly and of youngsters than is to be found in the local community, perhaps with a larger proportion of female than male, just ordinary folk, but to the eye of faith these are the community of grace who are our fellow pilgrims—a gift of God to us.

The community of grace is an essential component in Christian mission. In our spiritual understanding the community of the Trinity is the basic model of God. The Father loves the Son who returns that love, which then spills over into the whole of creation in the form of the Holy Spirit. We believe that we come to the Father, through the Son, in the power of the Holy Spirit. The whole community of God is involved in our experience of God and therefore it is not surprising if we also believe that this divine community is mirrored in the Church, the community of grace, as an essential part of our journey with God and to God.

A Christian is never alone. Even the Christian who is for the moment solitary is part of the community of grace, world-wide and history-long. We travel with a great company of grace: the apostles, saints and martyrs; the giants of the faith, Augustine, Aquinas, Luther, Teresa; those who formed our own heritage, Hilda, Cuthbert, Thomas More, Anselm; the Church reformers, Cranmer, Wesley, Newman; the social reformers, Elizabeth Fry, Wilberforce, Shaftesbury; the missionaries, Livingstone, Frank Weston, Roland Allen, C. F. Andrews; twentieth-century figures, Barth, Bonhoeffer, Temple; living exemplars, Mother Teresa, Desmond Tutu. We can all write our own list and perhaps we should, giving thanks for this community of grace which is as much our travelling companion on our spiritual journey as are the members of our local church or study group. The historical nature of this community of grace came home to us from one of the Eastern Orthodox participants of a recent World Council of Churches Assembly. He started his speech by saying 'When we met at Nicaea'. This second Council of the Church took place over twelve hundred years ago, but in the time-scale of God we are still the early Church, and the delegate was quite right in his taken for granted assumption that we and the Christians at Nicaea were members of the same community of grace getting on with the same business of the Lord.

It seems to us that there were nine significant elements in the life of the early Church.

- The church was a community open to all but particularly coming as a blessing to those who felt themselves to be unaccepted or humiliated in the society around, including women and slaves.
- The church had a care for people in need beyond its own group.
- It demonstrated an attractive fellowship.
- It proclaimed a clear simple message about what God had done in Jesus Christ.
- It practised a simple life-style; in the earliest days members had everything in common.

- Its members were prepared to suffer for the faith.
- It had a rich and satisfying prayer and worship life.
- It was open to God performing 'miracles' through its discipleship.
- Everyone of its members was a witness for the common belief.

If we are still members of the early Church then the elements of its life should still be found in our contemporary community of grace, the community called Church. The Church, a community of grace, must be a community with a purpose: holy, loving, and serving. The Church must be a community which believes that whatever the hardships or difficulties, we are all on the journey together, and God is with us.

We are called to travel with the community called Church. Perhaps the elements of life are not blindingly obvious when we look at the members of our local church, but perhaps they show up in a different way. The average church congregation will probably contain at least three types of Christians. First there are the 'ordinary' worshippers. They may well be living very draining, costly lives at home or in their places of work. Because of this they may come to the community called Church for support and low-key spiritual sustenance. Or some people may be at a very early stage in their spiritual journey, not yet prepared to give themselves to the faith with enthusiasm and commitment. They may be people who are tired, or at a stage where the faith has gone dim, so that they are treading water for a time and needing to be carried by their more faith-filled companions.

We once had the responsibility of organizing a community day in Canterbury. It was planned to involve all those who were serving the community in any way, including doctors, clergy, social workers, postmen and teachers. As we planned we realized that one group was under-represented, the trade union members. We decided to visit a trade union leader in his home and to ask him to join the community day. He listened to our sales talk and then he said 'You've come two weeks too late. It was my fiftieth birthday at the beginning of the month. My wife said to me "You've given twenty years of your life to serving others and getting them to union meetings. It's time somebody else took over." I decided that she was right, so we've taken up ballroom dancing.' We all have members of our community of grace who have been taken for granted for too long, and have now quietly laid down responsibility and have taken up the equivalent of ballroom dancing. They need to be nurtured and valued, we need their wisdom and experience. In the group of 'ordinary' worshippers there are also those who have a high regard for the Church's traditions. They are the guardians of past glories and they make a useful contribution to the contemporary Church; but there are some dangers. Nobody could have a higher doctrine of the traditions of the Church than the Russian Orthodox Metropolitan Anthony Bloom, but he has warned, 'Tradition is the living faith of the dead. Traditionalism is the dead faith of the living.'

Second, in our local community called Church there are those who are on fire with the Christian vision. They are the faith-filled disciples who involve themselves in the worship, teaching and study life of the Church. They are active in outreach and witness. They are likely to be most frustrated by those whose vision is limited to maintaining the present structures of the Church, or, because of past failures or demands, to ruling out new initiatives. The 'disciples' are a treasure, but the task of co-ordinating their energy and enthusiasm with the caution and traditions of the 'ordinary' worshippers is no easy task.

Then thirdly in the community of grace are the peace and justice people, who are particularly concerned with serving the needs of suffering humanity and campaigning on their behalf. They may well be a minority group in the average congregation and they may at times get themselves and others into hot water, but hot water also keeps us clean, and we need the abrasive challenge of their witness to remind us of the simple, sacrificial and outward-looking life-style of the early Church.

All these groups are likely to be found in the typical local church, but there will also be a global dimension in the life of such a church, for many congregations now have some kind of global link. The purpose of this link has changed in recent years. International links used to keep mission Churches overseas in touch with their mother Church in the West, and provide channels of communication and aid from mother Church to daughter Church.

But the world has changed. The first millennium might be regarded as that of the first Church, the Church of the East, when the early Church spread in ripples from Palestine to settlements around the Mediterranean world. The second millennium can certainly be regarded as that of the second Church, the Church of the West with its centre of gravity in Rome, Canterbury or Chicago. But the third millennium will undoubtedly be that of the third Church, the Church of the South and Far East, with its centre of gravity in Nairobi, Lagos, South America or Korea. Daughter Church is now self-governing, self-sustaining and self-propagating and has a wealth of wisdom to contribute to the Church of the West and of the East. Sometimes this wisdom comes with a jolt even when no criticism is intended. When a group of our Kenyan friends had returned to Kenya after they had spent one summer participating in a work project in England and visiting homes and congregations, we saw part of a letter which one of them had written to a friend. It went something like this: 'The Church in England is very strange. They always start their services on time, even when the Holy Spirit hasn't arrived!'

This brings us to the fourth element which was to be

found in Moses' journey to the promised land and in our journey with God and to God—glimpses of the promised land.

Glimpses of the promised land

Moses never entered the promised land, but God allowed him a glimpse of it when he climbed up Mount Nebo and looked across the whole area. In this way Moses was able to see that the vision which he had held for some forty years was no wish-dream, no castle in the air, but was real and solid—and his people would enter it and renew it.

We too have a vision of a world renewed for God by God and as we proceed on our journey of faith, sustained and orientated by springs in the desert, clarified and inspired by our walks with God, in companionship with the community of grace, we, from time to time, are granted glimpses of the promised land which confirm for us that our journey is no wish dream but is the most important thing in life or death.

Our worship is our primary place for getting glimpses of the promised land. For worship at its best is the world in tune. The objective of worship is not to convince heads by argument, but to lift hearts in wonder and awe to the divine source of grace and judgement. Through worship we are given a new vision, a new understanding, a new cause rich enough to use all that we are and all that we might become. Such worship is to be found in a local church that refuses to see itself merely as a gathering place for the elect or as an ark of salvation. The problem with being an ark of salvation is that it tends to make newcomers feel inadequate or even repelled. Our local church at its best is a welcoming place for all people, a place where they bring their births, marriages, deaths, their love for one another and their glimpses of vision to be touched and deepened and widened by the grace and judgement of God.

It is fashionable at the present time to look for mystical experience through inner journeys, through the explosion of light within. This has not always had a high priority in the Church. A story is told of a novice who once came to St Teresa to tell her about a wonderful religious experience which she had just had. 'Never mind', said the saint, 'keep on with your prayers and your work and it will soon go away.' Our spiritual forebears did well to be cautious. We now know that the part of the brain from which mystical experiences come is very close to that from which all kinds of mental delusions flow. As for everything else in our religion the test is 'Does this experience enable us to love God and our neighbours more effectively? Does it supply us with the will and the grace to do so?' If not, religious experience may be narcissistic self-indulgence and no better simply because it is clothed in religious clothing. The object of Christianity is neither to seek vision, nor to talk about it, but to live as Jesus once lived, and as he ever enables and empowers us to live.

The Church's worship, through word, and sacrament, through preaching, praise and prayer, modifies our inner soul-filled experiences by putting them alongside the images, rituals and teachings of the Church which over the centuries have proved to be effective in pointing Christians on their journey of faith. Worship then is controlled inspiration which gives us glimpses of the promised land without overwhelming our souls or destroying our minds.

For many people another opportunity for glimpses of the promised land on a journey of faith is through using our God-given power of thought. It has seemed incredible for some that Stephen Hawking's book *A Short History of Time* remained on the best-seller list for month after month. It does not seem strange to us for we believe that the search for an understanding of what lies beyond the stars, of what happened at the dawn of time, of what lies at the heart of the atom, is an exhilarating quest, close to the excitement which is awakened when we put our minds to the nature of God and God's purpose for creation.

This mind-stretching voyage of discovery is not without its dangers and confusions, however. Once you've seen the universe through the eyes of Einstein you can't forget what you know, although you might use Newton as a useful approximation sometimes. Once you have seen creation through the eyes of Darwin you cannot approach the creation stories of the Old Testament as history, although they can still be inspiring as a profound and poetic way of understanding the human condition before the awesomeness of God.

The Church of England's House of Bishops in its book *Christian Believing* expressed its belief that we must guard both the traditions of our faith and the process of exploration, whilst distinguishing between well-established beliefs and recent speculation. It is indeed our experience that exploring the boundaries of faith from a sure and certain core can be faith-strengthening and deepening.

The third place where we can get glimpses of the promised land is in the seeking after God in the lives of our fellow women and men. We were all moved by the images from the 'people's liturgy' in Liverpool following the Hillsborough football disaster. People came to the football ground and to the cathedrals and left behind their scarves, their hats, treasured programmes and bunches of flowers. Graciously, people for whom their football team was a source of community, pride and excitement allowed the Church to share their grief and confusion at the death and injury of their fellow supporters.

Sometimes the glimpse of the promised land is totally unexpected. We attended the opening of a new million-pound community centre converted from a large bus garage on a tough high-rise housing estate just inside the North Circular road in London. The great and the good had all been invited but unfortunately Prince Charles, who was to perform the opening ceremony, was delayed. To fill in the time, one of the organizers, a thirty-year-old Afro-Caribbean man, leapt onto the platform and started to tell us the story of the project.

He told of how he and his friends from the estate were together in gaol, not for the first time. How they had said 'There must be more to life than this'. How they had read the Bible together and had become faith-filled Christians. How they had pledged themselves to improve the lot of the youngsters on their estate when they were released from gaol. How they had had the vision of a community centre for the community, run by the community. How the bus garage had closed and how they had seen that this was the ideal building for such a centre. How they had prayed, cajoled, and persuaded local and national governments, trusts, institutions, Churches, and individuals to provide the necessary funds, whilst the group of brothers 'whose hearts God had touched' at the same time became committed members of one of the local black-led Churches. It was a story which gripped the audience, and humbled those of us who were Christians, by its fervour and faith. Then the Prince arrived, the speaker hopped from the platform and the official speeches began, but there was no doubt which speech would be remembered from that day, and it was not the ones on the programme. But our glimpses of the promised land are not always on the programme.

Often our glimpses of the promised land come from the undramatic lives of faith-filled Christians who quite unconsciously give us a peep at what is possible. We see a small congregation of urban Christians who are providing a gracious Christian village in the middle of an urban jungle. Their members are perhaps working long hours in the casualty unit of the hospital or on shift work at the local biscuit factory, yet they still find time to come to an early morning weekday service on the way to or back from work, take a pride in decorating the church at festivals, and bear one another's burdens, particularly in trying to keep the children of the community on the right lines when there is so much around to entice them into lives of danger and disaster.

It is through the lives of ordinary Christians like these that the faith is demonstrated as being credible and important. For at the end of the day the Church is its own religious evidence, its own demonstration of a world renewed for God, inasmuch as the love of God and of neighbour is abundantly in evidence through the life of a grace-filled community. There is a story told of when St John the Divine was on his deathbed, full of years, and his disciples came to hear his last message to them. He gathered all his strength and whispered 'Little children, love one another'. 'Yes, yes', they said, 'but you've said that to us before. What else have you got to say to us?' 'There is nothing else to say', said the saint, and quietly died.

Ideas and resources

Ideas

- Each member of a group may prepare a coat of arms with five sections. In four of the sections draw pictures or symbols which remind you of a time when you acted thoughtfully, emotionally, instinctively and intuitively. Meditate on your pictures and then in section five draw a final picture or symbol which summarizes all the others.
- Where have you met God in a new way? Write a prayer or a poem about your experience and perhaps about how it changed your direction.
- Write your own epitaph.
- Ask yourself, alone or in a group, what you need to do both within the next year and before the end of your life.
- Consider going on a pilgrimage with a group of fellow pilgrims for one or more days and try to include as many aspects of traditional pilgrimage as possible, i.e. worship by the roadside and in churches, sharing within the group readings from the Bible and other books, meeting with people along the way, learning about the places you pass, having a goal to arrive at. It is also a good idea to have an issue to focus on for the overall pilgrimage. (With careful planning it is often possible to arrange for a group to stay in parish halls.)

Group Bible study

Read Luke 24.13–35.

- Together tell the story of the events surrounding Good Friday through the perception of the disciples who had fled.
- Reflect on the times when you have felt insecure, lonely or in danger.
- How did the 'stranger's' interpretation change the disciples' whole understanding of recent history?
- When have you had your own perceptions changed through a new interpretation or experience?
- How do you understand the 'opening of the eyes' which came during 'the breaking of the bread'?

- What risks are you taking in your Christian discipleship, individually and as a group? What feeds you in your discipleship?

Resources

The National Retreat Association
24 South Audley Street
London WIY 5DL

Suggested reading

Vandana, *Gurus, Ashrams and Christians* (Darton, Longman and Todd, 1978)
Terryn Tastard, *The Spark in the Soul* (Darton, Longman and Todd, 1989)
Gerard Hughes, *Walk to Jerusalem* (Darton, Longman and Todd, 1991)
Adam Curle, *Tools for Transformation* (Hawthorn Press, 1990)

The genuine article

In the Decade of Evangelism some people fear that we will be battered by hard-sell evangelists striving to fill more pews in the right sort of churches, yet in fact creating even greater divisions in an already divided society. If that happens then the Decade will be a failure, for just as you don't fill a bath by turning the taps on more fully if there's no plug in the bath, so it's no use shouting a dogmatic Christian message more loudly into the ears of people already turned off by religion. But evangelism needn't be like that.

A friend of mine recently told me the story of a man who took early retirement and was finding time lying heavily upon his hands. A friend said to him, 'Why don't you start collecting pictures or antiques, that can be very satisfying. Look', he went on, 'I know someone who's an expert on Chinese jade, I'm sure he'd give you a few tips on collecting jade if you wished.' The man agreed and went to his first lesson. The expert gave him a piece of jade, told him to feel it and look at it carefully and then left the room. He came back half an hour later, took back the piece of jade, charged the man £25 and asked him to come back in a week's time. The same thing happened for six weeks, and finally the man complained to his friend, 'Look, you told me this chap was an expert, yet all he does is give me a piece of jade, tells me to examine it, leaves me with it for half an hour, and then charges me £25. I wouldn't mind so much, but last week's piece was a fake!'

I hope that the Decade of Evangelism will be a little like that. Not a piece of Christian hard sell, not basically about Church growth and development, but about human growth and development: an invitation for us all to handle for ourselves the treasure of God's goodness, truth, and love which Christians experience as being focused in Jesus of Nazareth. And then make our own judgement about what is true and what is a fake, in religion and in life.

When Billy Graham came to Britain, one of his large public meetings took place in the East End of London. He met with local church leaders to help him plan it. 'Where are your people at?' he asked. 'What shall I tell them?' Plenty of suggestions came, then a wise Roman Catholic said 'Tell them what you like, but be sure to tell them that God loves them, for that's what they need to hear'.

It might not be the official message, but that's a good thought for the day at the beginning of a Decade of Evangelism—'God loves us', that's what we all need to hear.